HEREFORDSHIRE CONSTABULARY 1857-1967

A History of the County Constabulary in Words and Pictures

Compiled by

VERA HADLEY

From the research of G.E. Forrest
and the photographic collection of E.A. Hadley

Published by:

Vera Hadley,
255, Whitecross Road,
Hereford, HR4. 0LT.,
U.K.

ISBN 0 9536792 0 9

British Library Cataloguing-in-Publication Data

A catalogue record for this book is available from the British Library.

Cover photograph reproduced by courtesy of
Mrs. J. Pike and Mrs. B. Barling, daughters of the late A. W. Death

FOREWORD

The late Mr. Robert McCartney had been aware of this project from the beginning, and was ready to give advice and his full support. As the last Chief Constable of Herefordshire his interest was important, and he had said that he would feel honoured to write a Foreword to this book.

Unfortunately, persistent health problems throughout this year, had prevented him from carrying out his intention.

Remembering the regard that Mr. McCartney continued to have for the Herefordshire Constabulary, and its officers and families, it is fitting that this book should be dedicated to him and to his four predecessors in the post of Chief Constable. Each, in his own way, made a contribution to the life and times of a small county Constabulary, and to over a century of policing Herefordshire.

INTRODUCTION & ACKNOWLEDGEMENTS

More than thirty years have passed since the Herefordshire Constabulary became a part of West Mercia Constabulary, and as time passes memories begin to fade. Much of what is described and pictured in this book happened long before any living memory, and the whole of what happened between 1857 and 1967 is history to younger generations.

Everyone who served in the county Constabulary in whatever capacity, has contributed to what is portrayed here, but without the resources made available to me by Gordon Forrest and my husband, Ted Hadley, I would not have attempted this project.

Gordon Forrest has had an interest in the Constabulary, and how it operated, since his early youth, and has done serious research into the subject for over forty years, resulting in a vast amount of information, of which I have been able to include only a small part.

A collection of photographs which started as a family album has grown to several hundred, thanks to the interest which Ted has maintained while he was in the police service and since his retirement, nearly twenty years ago. Many of the photographs are copies of those loaned by officers, former officers and their families. The quality of the photographs varied, from family snap-shots to studio portraits, but all were important in that they showed different people, changing times and fashions, as well as differing aspects of police life. There will inevitably be some disappointments, but it is hoped that an overall picture can be formed of a police service whose members had a pride in themselves, and in the county which they served.

Thanks are due to many individuals, notably to anyone who has added information and photographs from which this selection has been made. Gordon Forrest would like to acknowledge the assistance and encouragement received from the late Mr. R. McCartney, and for help given by the Librarian at the Police Staff College, Bramshill, and by the Home Office, Archives Section. Successive Chief Constables of West Mercia Constabulary, and their Chief Clerks, allowed Mrs. Gwen Parkes, before her retirement, to settle some research queries. More recently, Mrs Helen Marsh, of the Heritage Centre at Hindlip, has provided information from her sources. The former Librarian of Hereford City Library, Mr. B.J. Whitehouse, and present Librarian, Mr. D. Greaves, together with Mr. Robin Hill and staff of the Reference Section of the Library, have given help and advice whenever possible.

The past and present staff of Herefordshire Records Office, led by Miss S. Hubbard, have, for many years, given each of us invaluable, and cheerful, help and encouragement, and continue to do so, and further thanks go to Mr. D.H. Roberts, Mrs. G. Harding, for her interest, and Mr. D. Cousins, who has patiently read through what I have written. Mr. A. Bowden, of Orphans Press, has helped with any difficulties encountered along the way. There are many names left unmentioned, but the support of everyone, including Gordon's family, and in particular my own family, has been appreciated.

Vera Hadley
August 1999

CONTENTS

KEEPING THE PEACE IN HEREFORDSHIRE PRIOR TO 1857

The formation of County Constabularies in mid-Victorian times was the result of a slow process of evolution from the Anglo-Saxons, when the people of the country were responsible for their own discipline, and their tribal system ensured that every man was answerable for the behaviour of his own family and neighbours. Their allegiance to the king assured them of the 'King's Peace'. The Tithings and Hundreds of Alfred the Great became the shires, under the control of a Shire-reeve or Sheriff, and the system of 'Hue and Cry' was established, when all persons over twelve years of age were required to pursue a felon. The fore-runners of today's Justices of the Peace, the feudal Norman Lords of the Manor, in their turn, took over responsibility for law and order, and the position of constable (from the Latin 'comes stabuli '– master of the horse) came into use.

The Statute of Winchester, in 1285, brought together previous systems which had fallen into disuse, and 'Watch and Ward' was introduced in towns and boroughs. This meant that town gates had to be closed between sun-set and sun-rise, and watchmen could apprehend strangers. The Parochial police system, introduced in the reign of Elizabeth the First was based on the principle of making law enforcement an unpaid community responsibility, and was adopted in Herefordshire. The Constables were compulsorily elected by Vestry or Court Leet, and served for one year, carrying out Constabulary duties in addition to their own employment. It was sometimes the practice to pay someone else to take over if an individual did not wish to do it himself, therefore it was not always the person most suited to the job who actually carried it out. There was close association with the Justices of the Peace assigned to the particular Petty Sessional division, and eventually the appointment of Parish Constables became the responsibility of the Justices.

The high crime rate in London, in the early 18th. Century, led to the formation of the 'Bow Street Horse and Foot Patrol', instigated by Henry Fielding, a novelist and magistrate. These 'Bow Street Runners' became the first paid and uniformed Police service in this country. Despite protests from the population about loss of freedom, the Home Secretary, Sir Robert Peel, succeeded in 1829 in getting an Act of Parliament passed which allowed the formation of the Metropolitan Police, and this began the movement towards modern policing. Because of the ever-increasing growth of crime and unrest, and when the populace began to see the success of the Metropolitan Police, demands began for similar systems to be set up throughout the country.

In 1836 a County Commission on Rates made a scathing report on the Parochial Police throughout England and Wales, which, it alleged, was falling far short of the original Tudor concept, and the report said that Parish Constables were now being appointed from the lowest strata of society, uneducated and totally inadequate to perform their duties. A complete breakdown in law and order was resulting, and it was often the case that the Parish Constable, in his anxiety to keep a fine balance between enforcing the law, and retaining the goodwill of his neighbours when his year of office was over, was taking the easy option and doing as little as possible. By the legislation of the Municipal Corporations Act of 1835, those cities and towns which possessed a Royal Charter, were able to set up Watch Committees, and were required to form a police force, resulting locally in the formation of Hereford City Police and Leominster Borough Police in 1836. Generally, throughout the country, action was slow and by 1838 only about half of those boroughs required to do so had taken steps to set up their own policing.

A Royal Commission was set up in 1836, with one of the main contributors being Edwin Chadwick, who was well-known through his work on the Poor Law and the setting up of Union Workhouses. The report of the Commission in 1839 advised the setting up of County Constabularies in rural areas, but a motion put to Hereford Quarter Sessions to form a Police Force was defeated by thirty votes to twelve. A few Constabularies were formed in the first two years after the Act, including the neighbouring counties of Gloucestershire, Worcestershire and Shropshire, but nationally progress was slow, mainly because of financial considerations, and only twenty-eight rural constabularies had been established by 1855. Prior to the August 1839 Permissive Rural Police Act two of the small market towns of Herefordshire had taken steps to combat crime in their areas. Firstly in Ross, in 1838, under the guidance of a former Metropolitan Police officer, a small Force was established, and in Ledbury, early in 1839, when the citizens were having to cope with gangs of navvies quartered in the town whilst working on the Gloucester/ Hereford canal, two former Metropolitan police officers were recruited to help restore order. Both of these small Police Forces were financed by subscription from local land-owners and business men, who were paying for their own protection. In 1841 they were running out of enthusiasm, and money, and reverted to the former system of Court Leet.

Another attempt by a small town to police its own district was made by Kington Rural District in 1841, when a special Police Rate was levied, and under the Police Act of 1840, in conjunction with that of 1839, a Lock-up and residence for a Sergeant was built in the town. Robert Langdon who had served as a Sergeant in Birmingham became Superintendent, with Charles Rice Wilson as Sergeant, and two Constables, Henry Derry and James Gregg, who resided at Eardisley and Pembridge. In 1842 Percival Jefferson was appointed to cover the Byton and Coombe area, and Edward William Jones replaced Henry Derry. Initially the enterprise was effective, but as time went on support dwindled and many people from the surrounding villages resented paying for 'police we never see when they are wanted'. Complaints of this nature led to disbandment after nine years.

In 1842 the government passed the Parish Constables Act which contained two important provisions. The first of these made Constables more answerable to Quarter Sessions Authority, and the second allowed those counties with no established police force to appoint paid officers designated as Superintendent Constables. This was accepted in Herefordshire and at a meeting at the County Gaol, in September 1843, it was resolved that candidates should be not more than 42 years old, and at least 5 feet 7 inches tall and literate. They had to be married men with a wife of good character. The Superintendent Constables were paid not less than sixty pounds and not more than seventy five pounds per annum. These officers were responsible for policing the eleven Petty Sessional Divisions in the county, some with 25 parishes or more, and overseeing the unpaid Parish Constables who resided there, and were provided with a Lock-up house, together with a uniform and equipment, at the county's expense.

In April 1843 tenders were invited for the building of the first Lock-up in Sherford

Street, Bromyard and in 1844 it was occupied by John Marshall, a former Police Sergeant from Newent, Gloucestershire, who had 33 parishes in his area. Initially, his salary was £70 per annum, plus £20 to keep a horse, (cart provided), which by 1850 had risen to £75, plus an unchanged allowance for the horse. In the same year the Inspector of Prisons described the Bromyard Lock-up as being similar to that at Ledbury with 'slender' living accommodation for the Superintendent and his family. The ill-lit cells for the prisoners measured eight feet eleven inches by seven feet four inches, with a heating stove in the passage between them, which, even if lit for the whole day, failed to raise the temperature, because the heat escaped through two gratings in the wall. During the course of the year eighty-nine males and thirty females had been kept there for varying lengths of time, with, sometimes, an occupancy of eleven or twelve at the same time. Expansion of the system continued throughout the county and by 1856 the last Lock-up, together with a room for the Magistrates, was completed at Abbeydore, at a cost of four hundred and seventy pounds, making a total of ten Lock-ups, plus one at Hay, the expenses of which, and the services of the Superintendent, were shared with the Brecon and Radnor Authorities. During the twelve years before the formation of the full-time, paid Constabulary a total of twenty Superintendent Constables served the county, with no more than eleven serving at any one time, and there was no shortage of applicants for what was recognised as an important post. Experienced officers came from as far away as London and Lancashire, together with several from Gloucestershire and Worcestershire.

In 1841 the Chairman of the Quarter Sessions, Mr. John Barneby, put forward a proposal that a police force should be established in this county, but the proposal received insufficient support, and the matter was shelved. In 1853 Lieutenant-Colonel Morgan Clifford, MP, Chairman of Hereford Quarter Sessions, appearing before a Select Committee on County Policing, expressed his satisfaction with the Superintendent Constable method of policing, which was the least costly burden for the county. However, the die was cast, and following many Parliamentary debates, the Royal Assent was given to the County and Borough Police Act, on 21st. July 1856, making it compulsory for a Police Force to be set up in every county.

There is no doubt that this decision caused dismay and the suggestion was made that Herefordshire could continue to manage with the Superintendent Constables that it already had. However, the legislation came into force, and with it came the promise of grants payable to those forces which proved to be efficient, and consequently a Police Committee was appointed at the Hereford Michaelmas Sessions in October 1856. The Committee, together with representatives from Radnorshire met in the Shire Hall, Hereford, on the 8th. November 1856, under the Chairmanship of John Freeman, Esquire, and, after considering the needs of the county population of approximately 101,000, it was resolved to set up a Constabulary with the strength and pay structure as follows:

One Chief Constable at a salary of £280 per annum.
For expenses of every description £100 per annum.
(If the same Chief Constable is appointed for Radnorshire his salary to be £300 per annum, with expenses of £120 per annum).
Eleven Superintendents at £90 per annum.
For Horse, Saddlery and Travelling Expenses £30 per annum,

(with a cart and harness to be found by the County).

Eleven Sergeants at 21/- per week.

Twenty-two second class Constables at 17/- per week.

With the agreement of Radnorshire, who were to pay one quarter of his salary and expenses, the post of Chief Constable was advertised. There were sixty-four applications, including one from the Governor of Hereford Gaol, Captain James Drummond Telfer. At a committee meeting on 13th. December 1856, a short-list of three was agreed. These applicants were interviewed at the Epiphany Sessions, on 19th. January 1857, and Captain Telfer, was selected to be the first Chief Constable of Herefordshire and Radnorshire.

Rules and Regulations 'for the guidance of the new Constabulary Force' were presented to a meeting of the Police Committee, by the Chief Constable, on 21st. February 1857, and were approved after minor alterations, and it was left to the Chief Constable to decide the future arrangements for the horses and carts then being used by the Superintendent Constables. Other matters discussed were:

The Clerk was instructed to invite tenders for the supply of uniform clothing.

The matter of an office for the Chief Constable was discussed, and a suggestion was put forward that offices at the Shire Hall, shortly to be vacated by the Militia when they moved to their new barracks, might be suitable, subject to the rooms being made available when required, for the stewards of the Tri-ennial Music Festival.

It was recommended that 'the existing Station-Houses in the respective Divisions should be given up to the Chief Constable for the use of the new Force, and that a rent of two shillings per week be paid for the same, unfurnished, free from rates and taxes, to be deducted from the weekly pay of the Constable.'

'Justices Clerks of each Petty Sessional Division were to receive fees and allowances for duties performed by the new Constabulary Force, to keep a full, true and particular account of the same, and return them once in every quarter to the County Treasurer.....'.

A Rate of a halfpenny in the pound would be needed for Police purposes in the ensuing quarter.

The Clerk to the Committee, Mr. Corbett, 'would be allowed £5 per annum, for attending all their meetings, and performing other duties which might be required of him'.

The Superintendent Constables, whose posts were to become redundant, received their final payments and expenses, as follows: The two longest-serving, Superintendent Constables Shead, of Ledbury and Blossett, of Ross, each received twenty-one pounds, fifteen shillings and sixpence. Superintendent Constables Grubb, of Hereford, Dallow, of Bromyard, Dykes, of Weobley, Simpson, of Wigmore, Wilson, of Kington, Paine, of Dore, Langdon, of Leominster, and Durham, of Harewood End, each received nineteen pounds, eleven shillings and eight pence and Superintendent Constable Humphries, of Hay, a proportional payment of six pounds, twelve shillings and two pence.

Thus, the county was prepared for the inauguration of the Herefordshire Constabulary, and a new era in the protection of Law and Order was due to begin on 1st. April, 1857.

HEREFORDSHIRE CONSTABULARY
1857 – 1895

Captain James Drummond Telfer-Smollett
Chief Constable of Herefordshire, 1857 – 1895

Captain James Drummond Telfer, who was born on September 1st. 1824, was educated at the Royal Militia Academy, Woolwich, and from 1843 served with the Royal Artillery, reaching the rank of Captain. In 1854 he married Helen, the daughter of Colonel Jenkins of the Bengal Army, who was a widow with two daughters. A son of the marriage was born in 1855 at the County Gaol, Hereford, where Captain Telfer had become Governor on his retirement from the army in 1854. He was appointed as the first Chief Constable of Herefordshire on 19th. January 1857, and resided at 'Netherwood', Tupsley and later at 'Rosebank', Lugwardine. For eleven years he held the post of Chief Constable of Radnorshire jointly with his position in Herefordshire, until 1868 when Radnorshire appointed its own Chief Constable. In 1895, after thirty-eight years of service to the county, he succeeded to the family estates in Dumbartonshire, on the death of his cousin, P.B. Smollett, MP. He then added the name Smollett to his own surname and retired to Cameron House, Alexandria, where he died, aged 85 years, on the 27th. February 1909.

The first task of the Chief Constable was, of course, the appointment and location of the Superintendents, Sergeants and Constables who were to serve the county in the newly formed Constabulary. Consideration had to be given to the amount of previous experience, if any, of the individuals, and, whether married or single, accommodation had to be found for them on their respective beats. At the same time he was facing the same situation in Radnorshire, therefore a great deal of detailed planning was needed, calling for a person with exceptional organisational skills, which Captain Telfer proved to have.

The Chief Constable appointed seven of the former Superintendent Constables to the position of Superintendent in the Constabulary, and four officers who had transferred from Gloucestershire, Isle of Ely, Surrey and Northamptonshire made up the number required to cover the eleven Petty Sessional Divisions. One former Superintendent Constable retired on age grounds and another returned to his former occupation of game-keeper. The other two became Sergeants in the new Constabulary, whilst the other Sergeants, except one, came on transfer from other forces. The exception was Sergeant 33 George Groves, the last appointee, on the 25th. May 1857, to make up the initial strength, who came from the Royal Artillery at Woolwich, where he had gained experience in store-keeping and clerical work, and became the Sergeant/Clerk at Headquarters. Several of the Constables appointed had some previous police experience and the rest came from diverse trades and occupations, such as gardener, groom, butcher, shoe-maker, soldier, railway worker and a prison warder. Recruitment had not been completed when 1st. April arrived, and it was not until June that every officer was in his correct location for duty.

Disposition of Force – June 1857

Hereford Division
Supt. C. Briscoe, *Hereford*
P.S. 33 G. Groves, *Hereford, (Clerk)*
P.S. 1 C. Hopton, *Hereford*
P.C. 5 A. Spencer, *Wellington*
P.C. 17 J. Christy, *Eaton Bishop*
P.C. 10 W. Cope, *Hereford*
P.C. 29 W. Taylor, *Hereford*

Ross Division
Supt. E. Buridge, *Ross*
P.S. 20 J. Durham, *Walford*
P.C. 8 W. Vernall, *Ross*
P.C. 27 J.E. Cadwallader, *Upton Bishop*

Ledbury Division
Supt. G. Tanner, *Ledbury*
P.S. 21 T. Simpson, *Ashperton*
P.C. 13 T. Powell, *Coddington*
P.C. 15 T.G. Speirs, *Ledbury*
P.C. 18 J. Taylor, *Ledbury*

Bromyard Division
Supt. D. Harwood, *Bromyard*
P.C. 6 J. Williams, *Bromyard*
P.S. 3 S. Gregory, *Stoke Lacy*
P.C. 9 T. Kings, *Cradley*
P.C. 31 G. Christy, *Collington*

Whitney Division
Supt. C.R. Wilson, *Whitney*
P.C. 19 J. Lewis, *Dorstone*

Leominster Division
Supt. R. Dallow, *Leominster*
P.S. 32 W. Rowley, *Orleton*
P.C. 30 J. Jones, *Leysters*
P.C. 12 J. Bromley, *Stoke Prior*

Wigmore Division
Supt. W. Shead, *Wigmore*
P.S. 2 J. Jackson, *Leintwardine*
P.C. 26 F. Holsay, *Shobdon*

Kington Division
Supt. J. Humphries, *Kington*
P.S. 24 G. Winters, *Pembridge*
P.C. 7 J. Smith, *Kington*

Weobley Division
Supt. S. Langdon, *Weobley*
P.S. 25 J. Green, *Staunton-on-Wye*
P.C. 16 J. Webb, *Dilwyn*

Abbeydore Division
Supt. T. Blossett, *Abbeydore*
P.S. 23 W. Blunsdon, *Longtown*
P.C. 11 R. Davis, *Peterchurch*
P.C. 14 R. Ball, *Thruxton*

Harewood End Division
Supt. T. Dykes, *Harewood End*
P.S. 22 W. Vickery, *Marstow*
P.C. 4 G. Davies, *St. Weonards*
P.C. 28 J. Carver, *Much Birch*

As well as recruiting the officers required, Captain Telfer had to work out a systematic coverage of each beat, so that officers on adjoining beats met up with each other and with officers from the bordering counties of Gloucestershire, Worcestershire, Shropshire, Radnorshire and Breconshire. An officer's duty list became one of his most important possessions, and its loss could become a matter for a fine and suspension from duty until found. Some of the divisions were completely manned from the beginning, although accommodation was not settled immediately, as will be seen from the extracts in a later paragraph. Once the men were established at their stations the routine of police duties was carried out, as laid down in the rules and regulations drawn up by Captain Telfer. Some years later a Constable was fined five shillings for losing his instruction book, which he was ordered to replace by copying the rules and regulations into a 'small book'. Daily hours of duty were ten, seven of which were worked at night. General orders were issued at regular intervals and were read out at Divisional parades, likewise, pay was handed over and signed for at Divisional offices every fifteen days.

The first General Order, issued on 18th. April 1857, advised that:
'Each Superintendent on taking charge of the Division to which he has been ordered will be supplied with:-
2 Charge sheets,
1 Order book
1 Letter book
1 Report and Occurrence book,
1 Account book
He will make himself acquainted with the copy of the printed instructions of the Force.'

Captain Telfer did not hesitate to draw attention to any slackness, and from time to time warned the Superintendents as to their conduct and the example he expected them to set to the men in their charge. Very few of the original Orders exist, but in one case the early years are well documented in the Letter book of Abbeydore police station, and the daily life of Superintendent Thomas Blossett, who resided there, is clearly recorded. Thomas Blossett had been a beadle at Covent Garden, a Constable under the Duke of Bedford, a clerk at the House of Commons and a sailor before becoming a Superintendent Constable at Ross for fourteen years, and was known to be an outspoken individual, who nevertheless retained the respect of the magistrates. His Sergeant, who was stationed at Longtown, was William Blunsdon, with seven years previous police service in Wiltshire and Gloucestershire, prior to which he had been a guard on the Royal train when Queen Victoria travelled from London to Windsor. The two Constables in the division were Robert Davis, stationed at Peterchurch, and Richard Ball, stationed at Thruxton. Typical activities of the Superintendent mentioned in the book were: meeting officers at conference points, calling on local Magistrates for warrants, visiting cider and ale-houses, arresting prisoners and conveying them to court or gaol, attending Divine service and Sales and Fairs in the district, and reporting all events to the Chief Constable. Included among the entries were the following:

27th. April 1857
Arrived at Abbeydore with Sergeant Blunsdon and PC R. Davis. Took them on for duty at Longtown Fair.

11th. May 1857
PC R. Davis has taken a house at Peterchurch and has gone direct to his station with his goods from Hereford. Sergeant Blunsdon has taken a house at Longtown. It is undergoing repairs and will be ready in a few days.

13th. May 1857
Worked in the garden with Sgt. Blunsdon

June 1857
A house entered at Kingstone. Ball has been employed in the case but has not succeeded.

June 1857, in reply to the Chief Constable:
'with regard to PC Ball lodgings. I have not heard anything against the landlord, if it had been the case I would have reported it to you.'

In the early days of the constabulary the only permissible means of covering the beat, both in towns and rural areas, was on foot – 'pounding the beat.' A rural Constable would have seven or more parishes on his beat, which he was required to cover regularly and in all weathers. Let us reflect for a moment on this Constable, working a split ten hour day, without a day off except for one Sunday every five weeks, trudging mile after mile, with only his 'Bulls-eye' lantern to light his way at night. He had no means of carrying refreshment and if he was caught at one of his 'Ports of Call' he would face disciplinary action. His route from his station would be towards his first conference point, a place where, at a specific time, he would meet fellow officers to confer and pass on information and messages. As early as 1858 a Constable was dismissed for arriving at a conference point in a drunken state, and in September 1862 a Constable was fined one weeks pay for non-attendance at a conference point, and for making a 'shuffling' excuse.

It was possible that the Superintendent or Sergeant would also attend the conference point, so, unless he had a very good excuse to offer, the Constable had to be at the appointed place at the correct time. The senior officer, if present, would sign the officers pocket-books, and if no senior officer was present the Constables would sign each others book. This practice ensured that pocket-books were always kept up to date, and also served as a check on attendance at points. The same system of conference points carried on until the merger in 1967, but times and places were changed many times over the years, for obvious reasons. Before the age of the motor-car the Superintendent was allowed to use his horse and trap, and a rural Constable would sometimes contravene regulations and use a bicycle to reach the area of a conference point, hiding the bicycle behind a convenient building or tree, until the coast was clear and the senior officer had left. However, the Superintendent could be just as crafty and would offer the Constable a lift back to his station, thus ensuring that he had a weary walk back to collect his bicycle.

The first regular quarterly meeting of the Police Committee took place at the Shire Hall, Hereford in June 1857 and received the accounts to the 30th June 1857, which explained the income and expenditure of the Constabulary. The meeting went on to set a Table of Fees and Allowances to be payable for the execution of warrants, service of summonses, conveyance of prisoners etc., together with other allowances which were to be payable to all ranks for attendance at Sessions and Assizes.

REPORT OF THE POLICE COMMITTEE.

The Police Committee held their first Quarterly Meeting after the establishment of the Constabulary Force, on WEDNESDAY, the 17th of JUNE, 1857,

Present—

JOHN FREEMAN, Esq., in the Chair,

Edward Griffiths, Esq.
W. Bridgman, Esq.
Captain Peploe.
Robert M. Lingwood, Esq.
Rev. W. P. Hopton.
Rev. Edward Higgins.
Rev. Henry Dew.

The Receipts and Disbursements of the Chief Constable, together with the Vouchers, were laid before the Committee and allowed; a short summary only of which is subjoined, as the Report in full will be submitted to the Court:—

HEREFORDSHIRE CONSTABULARY POLICE ACCOUNT,

For the Quarter ending June 30th, 1857.

DR.	£	s.	d.	CR.	£	s.	d.
Rate made at Epiphany Adjourned Sessions, at ½d. in the Pound	628	0	7	Salaries	883	11	4½
Rate made at Easter Session at ½d. in the Pound	1254	8	4	Divisional Expenses	24	19	5½
Police Earnings	44	8	7	Formation	457	18	10
Rent of Stations, paid by Police Constables	9	7	8	Balance in hand	569	15	6
	£1936	5	2		£1936	5	2

The Committee recommend that notice be given to Mr. Thompson, the Inspector of Weights and Measures, that his services will not be required after Michaelmas Sessions, preparatory to placing those duties in the hands of the Police Force.

The Committee prepared the following Table of Fees and Allowances for the service of summonses and warrants, and the performance of other occasional duties which may be required of local Constables, subject to the approbation of the Secretary of State, according to the 3rd and 4th of Victoria, cap. 88, sec. 17 :—

TABLE OF FEES AND ALLOWANCES

To be taken by Constables appointed within the County of Hereford, under the Act of Parliament 3 and 4 Victoria, cap. 88, sec. 17, for the service of Summonses and execution of Warrants, and for the performance of other occasional duties which may be required of the said Constables, as settled at the General Quarter Sessions of the Peace, holden at Hereford, 29th June, 1857, subject to the approval of one of Her Majesty's principal Secretaries of State :—

	s.	d.
1. For service of a summons (including copy if necessary) on each person	1	0
2. For executing a warrant, or apprehending a prisoner on his own authority, each person	1	0
3. For executing a search warrant	2	6
4. For attending before a Magistrate to prove service or to prove case	1	0
5. Travelling *for any of the above purposes*, if more than two miles from the residence of the Constable, per mile, one way	0	6
6. For keeping in custody one prisoner, including his maintenance, per day	1	0
7. For conveyance of one prisoner (one way), per mile	0	6
8. For conveyance of two prisoners (one way), per mile	0	9
9. For conveyance of three prisoners (one way), per mile	1	0
For each prisoner above that number, 6d. each per mile.		
10. For any occasional duty performed under the orders of a Justice of the Peace, or of the Chief Constable, per day, not exceeding	5	0

But none of the above allowances are to apply or be made when the same are comprised in the Magistrates' Certificate of Expenses granted before Trial, pursuant to 7th George IV., cap. 64.

They also recommend that the following scale of payments be allowed to the Force for attendance at Sessions and Assizes, when such is required :—

Superintendents	2s. 6d. per day.	2s. 0d. per night.
Sergeants	2s. 0d. per day.	1s. 6d. per night.
Constables	1s. 6d. per day.	1s. 0d. per night.

Towards the end of 1857 HM Inspector of Constabulary, Captain Edward Willis, who had originally been an officer in the Lancashire Constabulary, and latterly Chief Constable of Manchester, made his first inspection of the Constabulary, and his report stated that the duties seemed to be well planned and the books well kept. He considered that the police stations were well provided with cells, equipped with heating appliances, although some stations and cells required alterations. However, he thought that the number of officers was insufficient for the requirements of the county and recommended to the Magistrates that there should be an increase of twelve men from the end of October 1857.

Wigmore Police Station.
One of the original Lock-ups and Petty Sessional Court buildings, taken over by Herefordshire Constabulary.

As with all new organisations, changes were inevitable and in May 1858 the Chief Constable considered that the shift system and supervision needed to be changed, and issued a General Order to that effect. He stated: '...The Chief Constable finds after due consideration that the system hitherto pursued with reference to the day and night patrols is totally ineffective so far as exercising any control over the men, at least over such as have any desire to evade their duty...' The Superintendents were given more discretion to arrange coverage of vacant beats. '...As a rule the ordinary scale of duty is three to four hours per day and five to seven hours per night, experience tells that in certain seasons, in certain localities, more day than night duty is necessary. The Chief Constable is therefore prepared to give the suggestions of each Superintendent every possible consideration. Five different weekly schemes will be necessary, to be numbered 1 to 5, and at the option of the Superintendent these may be taken in rotation week about or each for a fortnight or any one for two, three or four weeks at a time. But Superintendents must be alive to the necessity of the utmost vigilance on their parts...'

Throughout the early years wastage was high, partly because of the harsh working conditions which prevailed, and in many cases the men appointed were unsuitable for the requirements of the job. The following figures have been extracted from the appointments book, and cover the period from 1st. April 1857 to 31st. December 1859, (two years and nine months).

Number of officers appointed 1-April-1857 to 31-December-1859 - 109
(33 of these men had previous experience in 20 different police forces)

Resigned at own request	23
Dismissed for various reasons	14
Left to join another force	3
Died whilst serving	3
Still serving on 31-Dec-1859, but did not complete service	42
Continued after 31-Dec-1859, to retire on pension	17
Appointment did not take effect	7
Total	109

In January 1858 the eleven Superintendents were also appointed Inspectors of Weights and Measures and were instructed as to how they should publicise the day on which the weights and measures were to be checked, by the issue of printed notices, and the use of shop windows, where permitted. Thereafter, the Chief Constable included their activities in that capacity in his report to the Quarter Sessions, along with the crime returns, including the number of cases dealt with by the Justices, the number of indictable offences, how many persons had been committed for trial, fined or sent to prison. Convicts on ticket of leave in the county were also included. Finally the number of vacancies in the Constabulary, matters of superannuation, and eligibility for medical discharge grants were considered.

Another change took place in 1859, when two Superintendents posts were deleted. Whitney was absorbed into Weobley division, and Wigmore became part of Leominster division, although the courts remained in existence, with a Sergeant in charge of the station. By this means five Constables were added to the strength at very little extra cost, bringing the total manpower to sixty. In line with the increases in strength the Chief Constable was able to reward efficient service and good conduct by the introduction of classes in each of the three ranks, which meant that the pay structure could be varied. These 'rewards' also worked in reverse, as it meant that officers could be down-graded for a period, as a punishment for minor offences. The three-tier pay-scale of Superintendents in 1859 ranged from eighty two pounds per annum to ninety eight pounds per annum, according to the size of their division, and the two classes of Sergeant were paid twenty-one shillings or twenty three shillings per week. On recruitment Constables were categorised as second-class, receiving seventeen shillings per week, and were re-graded, at the discretion of the Chief Constable, to the top rate of nineteen shillings per week. These pay rates were still operative in 1864, and as a result of economic pressures more modifications took place in 1866 and 1873, until Constables were receiving two shillings and ten pence per day on joining, rising after one year to three shillings a day, and then by annual increments of one penny per day until the maximum of three shillings and six pence per day was reached. These rates were lower than those paid by surrounding counties, and it was not until 1891 that the Standing Joint Committee adopted a pay scale which was intended to attract more suitable applicants, who would provide a better service to the county.

The rules of discipline were unwritten, but the manner in which the men were expected to conduct themselves was laid down in orders to the Superintendents. Breaches of the rules, and other misdemeanours were dealt with by the Chief Constable, whose decision was final, with no recourse for the wrong-doer to appeal, either to the Police Authority or to the Home Office. Captain Telfer appears to have dealt with all offences in a very fair and even-handed manner, and minor offences were dealt with by stoppage of pay for a limited period, or reduction in class. These were severe measures, when taking into account the relatively low pay, any reduction was bound to cause hardship to the officer and his family, thereby punishing everyone in the household. Another means of dealing with misdemeanours was to require an officer to move to another station at his own expense, which again disrupted the whole family, as well as causing a knock-on effect and hardship to other officers and their families, who had to vacate their stations to make way for the offender. The most common reason for default was drunkenness, which in the first instance earned a caution, followed by dismissal if repeated. Absent from duty without leave, missing a conference point, not properly clothed and not being at home or lodgings when sick, are instances which occurred frequently. Some incidents which were recorded included:

1857. A PC dismissed when it was discovered that he had been in Hereford Gaol in 1854, for assault on a Hereford City police officer.

1857. A PC fined fifteen shillings for being drunk at the races and required to move to another station at his own expense.

1858. A PC dismissed for allowing a prisoner to escape, after leaving him alone for three hours.

1859. A PC fined twenty shillings for watching a fight take place, and not attempting to stop it or report it to his Superintendent.

1861. A PC whilst drunk assaulted his Superintendent, appeared in court and was fined ten shillings, with 14 days hard labour, and dismissed.

1862. A PC fined for running a foot-race at a fair and having sprained his ankle was made to forfeit his pay whilst on sick report.

1867. A PC dismissed for being under the influence of drink, disobeying orders from his superior and making water in a public place where he could be seen by passers-by.

Another officer, with a charmed life, accumulated the following record but survived in the service to draw his pension for seventeen years:-

1889. Fined one week's pay for losing his helmet on the way home from Hereford races, and to move at his own expense.

1890. Fined one week's pay for being under the influence, and promised to sign the pledge.

1893. Fined one week's pay for being in his station when he should have been out on duty.

1894. Fined one week's pay for being in a public house when on duty, and hiding from his Superintendent.

In 1862 the Inspector of Constabulary had reviewed all the station houses, and the court rooms which were incorporated in seven of them, and advised on necessary repairs and cleaning. One of the alterations he required was the provision of a separate entrance to the cells, to avoid using the same entrance as that to the Superintendent's house. At Ross he was concerned about an offensive smell coming from the pig-sty in the garden and requested its removal before his next visit. The station built at Sherford Street, Bromyard, in 1844, came under close scrutiny in 1864 when the state of the damp walls, due to seepage from the adjoining grave-yard was noted. Four years later, in 1868, the smell from the occupied cells proved to be most offensive to the Superintendent and his young family. Improvements to the standard of living of the residents was obviously in mind, when mention was made of the inconvenience caused to families by the unsatisfactory water supply at Harewood End and Wigmore. Satisfaction was expressed in 1869 that a new Police station with three cells and housing for the Superintendent, had been built at Ledbury, together with two cottages intended for Constables. Within six years a new station had been built at Bromyard which was regarded as being satisfactorily planned.

The police station at Old Gore, near Ross. A rented rural property, of good standard, occupied by the Upton Bishop Constable.

The duties of officers were again added-to in 1866 when they became Inspectors of Nuisances and of Lodging Houses, and were also expected to assist the Relieving officers. The Chief Constable was appointed Chief Inspector for ensuring the control of cattle plague and there were 70 prosecutions for breaches of these orders.

A summary of the strength of the force in 1867 showed that it consisted of forty-one married men, nineteen single men and one widower. Within the next few years two further Superintendent posts were dispensed with, when, in 1872 Harewood End became part of Ross division, and in 1875 Abbeydore became part of Hereford division. The rural population was gradually increasing, necessitating the formation of extra rural beats, and the presence of a local policeman began to be welcomed by the population, in contrast to the antagonism of the earlier years. The parishes of Bishops Frome, Linton, Lyonshall, Mansel Lacy and Ivington all now had their resident Constable, and a Superintendent's post was created at Head-quarters in 1876 when the Sergeant/Clerk was re-graded. The parish of Acton Beauchamp, being in a hop-picking area, made several requests to have its own Constable, but was always refused. The strength had now risen to seventy, at which level it remained for the next twelve years.

From the beginning of the Constabulary all members had contributed to the Superannuation Fund, and by 1870 this stood at two thousand, two hundred and sixty-two pounds, nine shillings and seven pence. At this stage no member of the Constabulary was receiving a pension, and no automatic right to one existed. Any application was considered by the Quarter Sessions, and at their discretion, a lump sum could be paid to an officer retiring on grounds of ill-health, or to a widow. An example of this occurred in 1864 when Superintendent Charles Hopton, of Ross, resigned due to illness and was paid the sum of fifty pounds, based on one month's pay for every year of service. Mr. Hopton, who had been the first officer to be appointed by Captain Telfer, and therefore the original police officer with the collar number HCC 1, died in 1865, aged thirty-six, leaving a widow and three children. The first pension from the fund was awarded in 1872 to Robert Dallow, of Weobley, a former Superintendent Constable, and the first Superintendent of the Herefordshire Constabulary to be based at Leominster, who retired on medical grounds and received an annual pension of fifty-four pounds and eleven shillings. In the same year Sergeant 17 John Christy, who had been incapacitated as the result of an injury, was awarded a pension of ten shillings and six pence per week. When the Pensions Act of 1890 came into effect on the 1st. April 1891 there were nineteen former officers receiving superannuation.

ROBERT DALLOW

He was born c.1811, at Grimley, Worcestershire.

Served with:
Birmingham City Police 1843-1849

Droitwich Borough 1849-1853

Worcestershire Constabulary 1853-1855

Superintendent Constable at Bromyard 1855-1857

Herefordshire Constabulary 1857-1872

He retired to live in Hereford, where he died in 1884.

Captain Telfer's report to the Quarter Sessions in October 1882, for the preceding quarter, explained how the various duties of the Constabulary had been carried out. During the period ninety-four people had been sent to gaol, and there were seven convicts on ticket of leave in the county, and five under police supervision. In the preceding year weights, measures and scales of five hundred and ninety-nine persons had been checked, resulting in forty-one fines and three persons ordered to pay costs. The Chief Constable then begged for '...the favourable consideration of the court, the case of Superintendent Thomas Dykes, who is upwards of sixty-one years of age, and is reported medically unfit for further service. Superintendent Dykes has discharged the duties of Superintendent for twenty-five and a half years, since the establishment of the Police Force, in a very efficient manner, and I regret he is unable to continue in the service...' He also mentioned PC 29 George Hill, with seven years and nine months service, who was suffering from deafness brought on by exposure to night air. Superintendent Dykes was awarded a pension of four shillings and nine pence farthing per day, and PC Hill was granted a gratuity of twenty pounds. A pension had previously been granted to former PC 35 Cornelius Baynham for one year only, and was now extended for a further three months.

Throughout the country in 1887 there were two hundred and thirty one police forces in existence, but the Local Government Act of 1888 which abolished those forces serving a population of less than 10,000, meant the end for forty-eight of the one hundred and seventy-two Borough forces, including Leominster Borough Police. Therefore, on the 1st. April 1889 the Leominster force merged into Herefordshire Constabulary, the Superintendent, George Johnson, received a pension from March 31st., and the Sergeant and six Constables moved to Burgess Street police station under the jurisdiction of Superintendent Richard Strangward, of Leominster and Wigmore division. The former Leominster Borough police station in New Street, Leominster was vacated. Also, by legislation of the same Local Government Act, the business formerly conducted by the Police Committee at Quarter Sessions passed to the Standing Joint Committee of the newly constituted Herefordshire County Council.

LEOMINSTER BOROUGH POLICE,
at 31st. March, 1889
Standing, L. to R: PCs C. Rooke, J.J. Thomas, M. Crump, W. Blunsdon, H. Daymond, S. Williams,
Seated: Sergeant T. McNaught, Superintendent G. Johnson

The merger of the two forces increased the establishment to seventy-seven, one Chief Constable, eight Superintendents, thirteen Sergeants and fifty-five Constables, and collar numbers HCC 62 to 68 came into use for the first time. One Superintendent was Chief Clerk at Headquarters, and seven were in charge of Divisions. The thirteen Sergeants were allocated as follows: Hereford, Ross, Ledbury and Bromyard, one each, Leominster, two, and four to section stations at Whitney, Wigmore, Harewood End and

Abbeydore. These four Sergeants were responsible for their own beat and also supervised the Constables on adjacent beats, and this supervisory role usually ensured their promotion to Superintendent. The three remaining Sergeants were based on large rural beats, at Dilwyn, Eardisley and Cradley. The fifty-five Constables were based in Hereford and the market towns and on forty rural beats.

Superintendent Richard Edwards retired from Kington in 1891, and thereafter Kington became a section station within Weobley Division, leaving a Sergeant in charge at Kington. The total strength of the force now increased to seventy-nine by the addition of two Constables. The introduction of a new weekly pay scheme, together with the provisions of the Pensions Act, began to make future prospects appear brighter for the long-service officer. The first applicant for a pension under the Police Act of 1890, was the Deputy Chief Constable, Superintendent William Cope, aged sixty, who had been appointed in March 1857, and had risen through the ranks to become a Superintendent, being appointed Deputy Chief Constable in 1880, the first man to hold the position. His application for a pension in April 1891, stated that his annual rate of pay was then one hundred and fifty pounds, thirteen shillings and ten pence, and he applied for a pension of one hundred pounds, nine shillings and two pence. The Chief Constable approved the claim and stated that Mr. Cope '...was not absent from actual efficient service through his misconduct, neglect of duty or sickness resulting from his own default, or from injuries caused by his own default...' this being the wording of the Act which entitled the applicant to claim a pension. The Act laid out the conditions to be met, including the fact that no Constable or Sergeant under fifty years of age, or Superintendent under fifty-five years should be entitled to retire on pension, other than on medical grounds, and stipulated the scale of pensions according to years of service.

William Cope, was born in Bosbury, Herefordshire in 1832, appointed Constable in March 1857, promoted Sergeant in 1858, and Superintendent in 1868, and was Deputy Chief Constable from 19-6-1880 to 4-4-1891. From his family of eleven children two of his five sons also became Superintendents, William Cope in the Worcestershire Constabulary, and Andrew Cope in the Herefordshire Constabulary. Mr Cope died on 15th. May 1897.

The new pay scales for serving officers, proposed from 11th. July 1891, were as follows:-

'First Class Superintendents an addition of 1/9 per week for each period of 3 years service, up to 12 years inclusive.
Second Class Superintendents an addition of 1/9 per week after 3 years service.
Third class Superintendents no addition.

First Class Sergeants an addition of 1/2 per week after 3 years service.
Second Class Sergeants an addition of 7d. per week irrespective of service.
15 Police Constables now serving, an addition of 1/9 per week after 10 years service.
16 Police Constables now serving, an addition of 1/2 per week after 4 years service.
14 An addition of 7d. Per week under 4 years service.
In future Constables to commence at £1. 1s. 0d. per week, rising by annual increments of 7d. Per week up to £1. 6. 3d. per week.'

'The actual present effect of these additions is shown below.'

			Present Weekly Pay—each.			Total Present Weekly Pay.			Proposed addition per week.			Future Weekly Pay.			Total Future Weekly Pay.			Total Men.
Superintendents :	1st class	1 of 12 years service	2	10	2	2	10	2	...	7	...	2	17	2	2	17	2	1
	„	... 1 of 6 years ditto	2	10	2	2	10	2	...	3	6	2	13	8	2	13	8	1
	„	... 1 under 3 years ditto	2	10	2	2	10	2	...	..	...	2	10	2	2	10	2	1
Ditto	2nd class	... 1 of 3 years ditto	2	6	8	2	6	8	...	1	9	2	8	5	2	8	5	1
	„	... 2 under 3 years ditto	2	6	8	4	13	4	...	...	...	2	6	8	4	13	4	2
Ditto	3rd class	... 1 „ „ „	2	3	2	2	3	2	...	...	...	2	3	2	2	3	2	1
Sergeants :	1st class	... 2 of 3 years ditto	1	9	9	2	19	6		1	2	1	10	11	3	1	10	2
	„	.. 5 under 3 years ditto	1	9	9	7	8	9	...	...	...	1	9	9	7	8	9	5
	2nd class	... 7 „ „ „	1	6	10	9	7	10	...	...	7	1	7	5	9	11	11	7
Police Constables :		... 15 of 10 years ditto	1	4	6	18	7	6	...	1	9	1	6	3	19	13	9	15
		6 of 4 years ditto	1	4	6	7	7	...	...	1	2	1	5	8	7	14	...	6
		3 of 4 years ditto	1	3	11	3	11	9	...	1	2	1	5	1	3	15	3	3
		5 of 4 years ditto	1	3	4	5	16	8	...	1	2	1	4	6	6	2	6	5
		2 of 4 years ditto	1	2	9	2	5	6	...	1	2	1	3	11	2	7	10	2
		... 3 under 4 years ditto	1	2	2	3	6	6	...	...	7	1	2	9	3	8	3	3
		4 „ 4 years ditto	1	1	7	4	6	4	...	...	7	1	2	2	4	8	8	4
		... 7 „ 4 years ditto	1	1	...	7	7	...	...	...	7	1	1	7	7	11	1	7
		... 4 „ 4 years ditto	1	1	...	4	4	...	...	...	...	1	1	...	4	4	...	4
		... 8 „ 4 years ditto	...	19	10	7	18	8	...	1	2	1	1	...	8	8	...	8
Grand Total .. 78			...	...	...	101	...	8	...	...	...	...	...	...	105	1	9	78

In 1894 extra duties were carried out by six Superintendents and five Sergeants who received two shillings and sixpence per case, up to a maximum of ten shillings per week, under the Contagious Diseases (Animals) Acts. Six Superintendents and one Sergeant had duties laid down under the Explosives, and Food and Drugs Acts, and four Superintendents and one Sergeant acted as assistant relieving officers, receiving allowances ranging from ten pounds to four pounds per annum. The annual inspection of the Constabulary again found that uniforms and appointments were in good order, and the books and returns well kept. Station houses were recorded as being clean and in good order, and the management, numbers and discipline of the force efficiently maintained. Eight members of the force were proficient in First Aid and held certificates of the St. John's Ambulance Association.

The growth of the police service in the county during the thirty-eight years of

Captain Telfer's auspicious tenure of office meant that, as his retirement approached in 1895, he would leave behind him a firm, solid base upon which his successor could build in the future. The Constabulary prepared itself for progress, and the changes which were envisaged under a new Chief Constable.

HEREFORDSHIRE CONSTABULARY 1895 – 1923

Captain the Honourable Evelyn Theodore Scudamore-Stanhope Chief Constable of Herefordshire, 1895 – 1923

Captain Stanhope was born on the 9th. January 1862 and educated at Wellington College. He served with the 60th. Rifles in Natal, Egypt, Malta, Soudan and Cyprus from January 1881 to October 1887, before joining the Army Service Corps with whom he remained until April 1895, when he was attached to the Staff of His Excellency the Governor of Malta. He had married, in 1888, Julia Dasha, the daughter of John Gerald Potter, of Darwen, Lancashire. Captain and Mrs. Stanhope resided at Nupton House, Aylestone Hill, Hereford. He retired from his post in Herefordshire in 1923, on the grounds of ill-health, and died in France in 1925. He was buried at Holme Lacy, Herefordshire, where he had family connections.

Captain the Honourable E.T. Scudamore-Stanhope was the successful applicant from amongst those who had responded to the advertisement placed by the Standing Joint Committee in March 1895, and he took up his duties on 27th. April 1895. His twenty-eight years service with the Constabulary, beginning as the Victorian age drew to a close, through the Boer War and the Edwardian era, continued through the upheaval of the First World War, and into the years of peace and recession which followed. The new Chief Constable was a man of autocratic manner, and a strict disciplinarian, but most of the major changes which took place in the police service in the county during his years of office were as a result of national legislation rather than any sweeping changes made by Captain Stanhope, indicating that he was satisfied with the 'status quo', and that he took over a Constabulary which had been left in good order by his predecessor.

Police duties carried on in the normal way, and a General Order issued in 1896 emphasised the unchanged system of conference point and foot patrol.

> 'No Sergeant or Constable is to use his Bicycle on duty without Permission from the Superintendent or Sergeant in charge of his division, excepting in Cases requiring Prompt action, such as immediate pursuit of thieves &c.
>
> They will on no account be used by Sergeants or Constables going out on their ordinary tour of duty.
>
> No Sergeant or Constable is ever to appear on a Bicycle in uniform.'

Large civil-engineering works going on in the county indicated the need for more police personnel in those areas, and three extra Constables were appointed. After a very troubled start, work was under way on the Bromyard – Leominster railway line, and PC 46 J.H. Williams was transferred to Hatfield. PC Williams had joined the Constabulary in 1892 and eventually became Superintendent at Ledbury before his retirement in 1923. In the north of the county the water pipeline from the Elan Valley, in mid-Wales, to Birmingham was under construction in the Leintwardine area, with large gangs of engineers and labourers at work. Two Constables were moved into the area in 1898, to cover the beats of Brampton Bryan and Downton.

WALFORD POLICE STATION

An innovation, in 1896, had been the introduction of fifty of the familiar large notice-boards outside police stations, intended to draw the attention of the public to any items of interest or information.

The '...unsuitable nature of the Chief Constable's offices of this county...' was the subject of a letter from Captain Stanhope to Sir Richard Harrington, the Chairman of the Standing Joint Committee, in September 1897. The content of the letter pointed out that there were four rooms, the first of which '...is used as an office, the second as an enquiry office and a room for the Constables on duty, as well as a room in which Constables of the Hereford Division can write reports and see information when in Hereford. The third room is used as a waiting room and dining room for Constables coming in on duty at Assizes, Sessions &c, and the fourth room as a store room...' In the opinion of the Chief

Constable it was essential that there should be an officer undergoing training as a Clerk, as the present Clerk was in his fifty-seventh year, had over thirty-eight years service, and was entitled to leave at any time, on pension. He found that it was not possible to accommodate a trainee, as at the time he was himself sharing an office with the Clerk, and the other rooms were all too dark to use as offices. In addition all the rooms were '...much affected by damp...... in consequence of their being built on the ground and having no damp-course. There is a smell of foul air on opening the doors in the morning...' and '... the store-room is so damp that clothing and leather quickly go mouldy. The dining room is very dark, the bottom of the windows......... five feet from the ground...' He went on to describe the unsatisfactory situation at the County Police Station, which was sited at the County Gaol, in Commercial Road, Hereford in these words, '...With the exception of the kitchen the Superintendent has only one room in which to do his office work, take charges and give instruction to the men of his Division, consequently he is obliged to use this room as a private sitting room...' Captain Stanhope went on to say that he thought it would be possible and desirable to build on a suitable room, at the Police Station, to be used as an office and dining room for the men, in which they could also write reports and carry out the usual daily duties. He finished by pointing out that the Police Station was the proper place for a room of this kind, and not as it was at the time, in the Chief Constable's offices.

At the next meeting of the Standing Joint Committee it was resolved that the County Surveyor should submit a report on the matter and in due course he estimated that a new building would cost nine hundred and fifty pounds. In March 1898 the County Surveyor was instructed to prepare plans for the proposed building, at a cost not to exceed eleven hundred pounds, to be erected at the left-hand side of the Shire Hall forecourt, adjoining a house for the Superintendent, facing onto Union Street, and to accommodate both the Chief Constable's offices and the Hereford Divisional Police Station and cells. In July of that year the estimate of Mr. Cooke, Builder, was confirmed and a contract agreed for a building to cost one thousand, four hundred and ninety-six pounds. Eventually, when everyone was settled into the new premises an extra Constable was appointed to work alongside the Clerk, followed four years later by another Constable as a Reserve.

In 1900 nineteen officers from all parts of the county attended a course of First Aid lectures given in Hereford by Doctor E.W. DuBouisson, sixteen of whom were successful in gaining Certificates of the St. John's Ambulance Association, and were subsequently issued with three badges each to be attached to uniforms. Fifty three officers were now qualified to render First Aid.

A General Order of 1903 proclaimed that 'Drunkenness so unfits a man for his highly responsible office of Constable that in no case will this Chief Constable pass over the offence when committed on duty'. Sergeants and Constables were forbidden to accept refreshments of any kind, when on duty, from any person whatsoever, and any breach reported would be severely dealt with. Officers were required to make a copy of these orders and 'gum it into his instruction book'. Instructions were also given that in future, when an officer was under orders to move stations, three estimates must be obtained for the removal, and the Superintendent would decide which one should be accepted. Occupants of rented accommodation were also reminded that they were responsible for internal up-keep and that it should be inspected quarterly, by the Superintendent. Hitherto the police had been exempt from Licence duty in respect of carriages used solely for official duties, but this concession was withdrawn by the Board of Inland Revenue in 1906, so henceforth Superintendents were required to take out a licence for their police carts.

The Inspector of Constabulary after his inspection of Police Stations had drawn attention to the poor lighting in some of the cells, and arrangements were made, where a gas supply was available, for lighting to be installed. An earlier recommendation had been that all cells should be fitted with a battery operated bell so that the occupant could summon the officer in charge. Plans were drawn up for a new court room at Ross, and a cottage for the Sergeant was built at a cost of four hundred and eighty-four pounds. Drainage and sanitary repairs to the Superintendent's house at Leominster cost twenty-four pounds, and at Bromyard general repairs to the Superintendent's house cost over seventy-one pounds, with a hot water system costing another four pounds eight shillings and six pence.

A new Instruction book for the guidance of the members of the Constabulary was issued in 1906 and the first page detailed a General Order reminding 'Members of the Force... that the character of a body is, not unfrequently, judged by the conduct of individuals, and it will consequently be the interest of the zealous and well conducted of all ranks to assist in bringing to the Chief Constable's notice any irregularity or neglect of duty on the part of others'.

Pay scales, allowances, guidance about Leave of Absence, Pensions and Conditions of Service were all included. The following items from the Conditions of Service are of interest:-

1. Every Constable shall devote his whole time to the Police Service; serve and reside wherever he is ordered, and not receive a Lodger without the sanction of the Chief Constable; promptly obey all lawful orders, conform to all regulations, and perform all other duties that may from time to time be required of him.

8. He will be required to have in his possession a respectable suit of plain clothes.

10. He shall at all times appear in the established Uniform, unless otherwise directed, and be always clean and neat in his person and dress.

22. He shall not enter a Public-house, Beer-house, or place for the sale of Liquor, unless for the purpose of restoring order or in the execution of his duty, or in order to obtain necessary refreshments, and in either case will remain no longer than is absolutely necessary for the purpose. He is also strictly prohibited from borrowing money or receiving drink, or being in any way indebted to Publicans or Beer-house Keepers.

24. Wherever the word 'Constable' appears in these conditions, it shall be understood to mean equally, if necessary, 'Superintendent' or 'Sergeant'.

The book also contained a copy of 'An Address to Police Constables on their duties' by the Honourable Sir Henry Hawkins, one of her Majesty's Judges, reprinted from the 'Police Code and Manual of the Criminal Law'. Some points are worth noting:

Conduct on Duty:...you must, when on duty, allow nothing but your duty to occupy your thoughts. You must studiously avoid all gossiping....... .

Vigilance:...constant endeavour by your vigilance to prevent crime.....and not by your negligence tempt others to commit it.....

Meddlesomeness: Beware of being over-zealous or meddlesome. These are

dangerous faults.
Discretion:...be very careful to distinguish between cases of illness and drunkenness.
Good Temper:....keep a curb on your temper....be civil and listen respectfully....
Obedience:...let me impress upon you the necessity of absolute obedience to all who are placed in authority over you, and rigid observance of every regulation made for your general conduct......
He continued by giving sound advice on questioning, advised writing down conversations word for word, and emphasised the importance of telling 'the whole truth'.

A huge benefit was given in 1906 when an extra day off in every five weeks was granted, making two days in all. However, this could not be taken between 15th. July and 15th. October when a large influx of casual workers from the Midlands and South Wales came into the area for hop-picking, at which time some Constables were temporarily moved from their own station to assist the local officers in the hop-picking areas. From 1912 onwards a Police Reserve, who received a retainer of two pounds per year, could be called upon at hop-picking time, or in any emergency situation. The Weekly Rest Day Act which had been passed in 1910, but was not implemented in Herefordshire until 1914, meant that because of the extra time-off, more man-power was needed to keep up the same standards, and another Sergeant and six Constables were appointed.

A King's Medal was instituted by King Edward the Seventh in 1909 as a reward for 'good service, instances of conspicuous devotion to duty, and heroic acts of courage' by police officers and firemen, and in 1910 the Standing Joint Committee granted approval to a request by the Chief Constable that the particulars of a case of courageous conduct on the part of PC 67 David Thomas should be submitted to the Secretary of State for consideration of a retrospective award. PC Thomas had been attacked at Shobdon in December 1906, and, with assistance, had apprehended his attacker.

The out-break of war in 1914 had an immediate effect, when five reservists were called to the Colours on the 4th. and 5th. of August, including both of the Constables from Bromyard town, PC 78 A.R. ('Gun-boat') Smith recalled to the Royal Navy, and PC 29 E. Jarrett to the Kings Shropshire Light Infantry, along with three others, PC 64 B.C. Hardwick from Hoarwithy and PC 57 W.J. Wadham from Kington, who both went to the Royal Artillery, and PC 56 J. Thomas from Ledbury, to the Grenadier Guards. Initially, there was no automatic right of return to the police service at the end of hostilities, so men were recruited to fill the vacancies, along with the First Police Reserve, so that by the end of August the full establishment had been regained. Later, Sergeant 15 H.C. Reynolds, of Hereford, and PC 40 D. Evans, of Pontrilas, who were both former soldiers, were seconded to Shrewsbury Barracks as Drill Instructors. Five more members of the Police Reserve returned to full-time duty in 1915 after fifteen constables had enlisted in the Army, all police recruitment ceased, and one thousand, five hundred and thirty-nine civilians in the county registered their willingness to serve as Special Constables.

A total of thirty-one men served in the armed forces during the war and by the cessation of hostilities the Constabulary was operating with only sixty men.

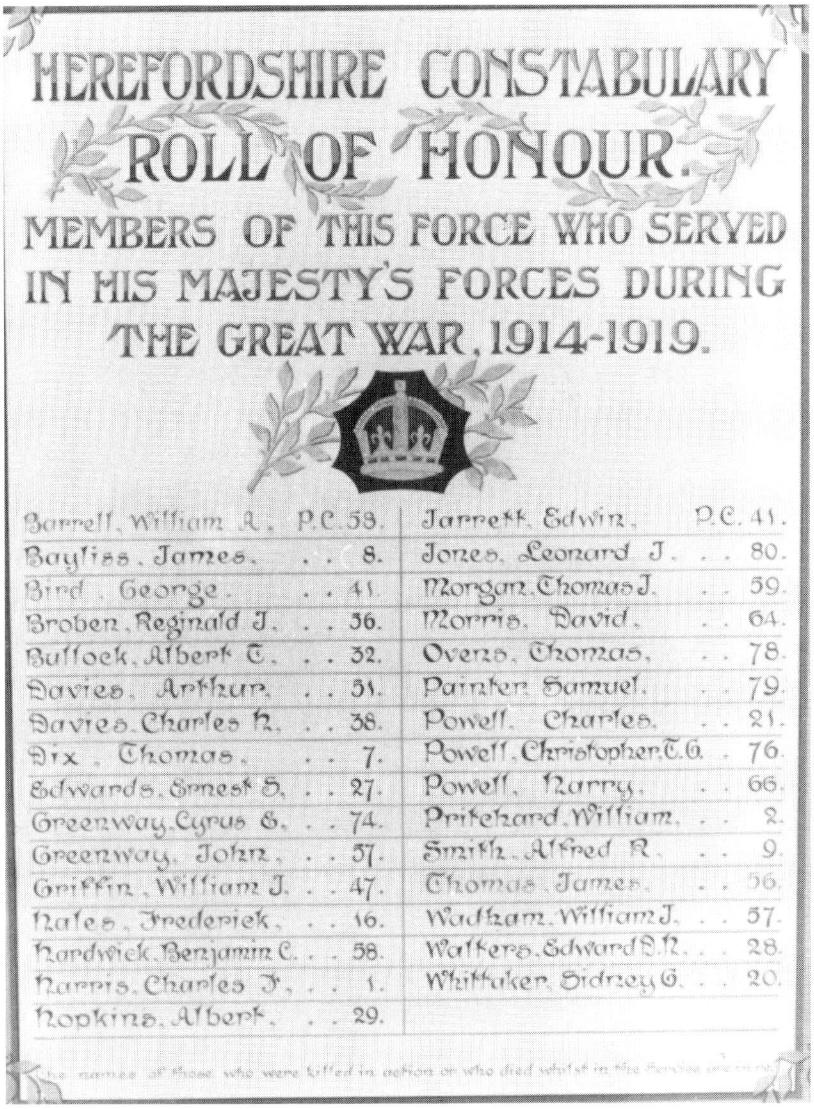

HEREFORDSHIRE CONSTABULARY

ROLL OF HONOUR.

MEMBERS OF THIS FORCE WHO SERVED IN HIS MAJESTY'S FORCES DURING THE GREAT WAR, 1914-1919.

Name	P.C.	Name	P.C.
Barrell, William A.	58.	Jarrett, Edwin.	41.
Bayliss, James.	8.	Jones, Leonard J.	80.
Bird, George.	41.	Morgan, Thomas J.	59.
Broben, Reginald J.	36.	Morris, David.	64.
Bullock, Albert T.	32.	Ovens, Thomas.	78.
Davies, Arthur.	51.	Painter, Samuel.	79.
Davies, Charles H.	38.	Powell, Charles.	21.
Dix, Thomas.	7.	Powell, Christopher, T. G.	76.
Edwards, Ernest S.	27.	Powell, Harry.	66.
Greenway, Cyrus S.	74.	Pritchard, William.	2.
Greenway, John.	57.	Smith, Alfred R.	9.
Griffin, William J.	47.	Thomas, James.	56.
Hales, Frederick.	16.	Wadham, William J.	57.
Hardwick, Benjamin C.	58.	Walters, Edward D. H.	28.
Harris, Charles F.	1.	Whittaker, Sidney G.	20.
Hopkins, Albert.	29.		

Three officers lost their lives in the conflict,
PC 58 W.A. Barrell, PC 41 G. Bird and PC 56 J. Thomas.

Two men had returned before the end of the war, three others were declared medically unfit to resume police service, and twenty-three awaited demobilization. Several of the long-serving officers who had been retained for the duration expressed a wish to retire, so, even if all those who had served with the military wished to return, there would still be vacancies for other ex-servicemen wishing to apply.

On the 1st. January 1919 there were eight auxiliary officers still serving:

Reserve Sergeant A1 E. Dance, *Ross*
Reserve Sergeant A2 G. Ellis, *Ledbury*
Reserve Sergeant A3 A. Protheroe, *Hereford*
Reserve Constable A5 B. Vearnalls, *Ledbury*
Reserve Constable A7 W.G. Booton, *Bromyard*
Reserve Constable A8 H.A. Lloyd, *Leominster*
Reserve Constable A9 J. Bethell, *Hereford*
Reserve Constable A12 J. Morris, *Weobley*

Herefordshire Constabulary.

SCALE OF PENSIONABLE PAY, 1st OCTOBER, 1918.

RANK.	PERIOD.	PAY PER WEEK.			ALLOWANCES.
		£	s.	d.	
CONSTABLES	On appointment .. .	2	0	0	Clerks to receive additional pay as follows:—1/2 (s. d.) for each week during the first 5 years of service; 1/9 (s. d.) each week during the next 5 years of service, and 2/4 (s. d.) each week after 10 years of service.
,, ...	After 1 years' service ..	2	1	0	
,, ...	,, 2 ,, ,, ..	2	2	0	
,, ...	,, 3 ,, ,, ..	2	3	0	
,, ...	,, 4 ,, ,, ..	2	4	0	
,, ...	,, 5 ,, ,, ..	2	5	0	
,, ...	,, 6 ,, ,, ..	2	6	0	
,, ...	,, 7 ,, ,, ..	2	7	0	
,, ...	,, 8 ,, ,, ..	2	8	0	
,, Merit Class ..	,, 15 ,, ,, ..	2	9	0	The increases after 15 and 20 years' service respectively are dependent on certificate of good conduct.
,, ,, ,, ..	,, 20 ,, ,, ..	2	10	0	
SECTION SERGEANTS	On appointment	2	13	0	
,, ,, ...	After 1 year	2	14	0	
,, ,, ...	,, 2 years	2	15	0	
,, ,, ...	,, 3 ,, ,, ..	2	16	0	
,, ,, ...	,, 4 ,, ,, ..	2	17	0	
STATION SERGEANTS	On appointment	3	4	0	
,, ,, ...	After 1 year	3	5	0	
,, ,, ...	,, 2 ,, ...	3	6	0	
,, ,, ...	,, 3 ,, ...	3	7	0	
		Per	annu	m.	
SUPERINTENDENTS	On appointment	200	0	0	
,, ...	After 3 years	210	0	0	
,, ...	,, 6 ,, ...	225	0	0	
,, ...	,, 9 ,, ...	240	0	0	
,, ...	,, 12 ,, ...	255	0	0	
DEPUTY CHIEF CONSTABLE ..		20	0	0	Additional.

WAR BONUS: All Ranks to receive 9/4 (s. d.) per week each, with 1/- (s.) per week additional for each child under 14 years of age until the end of the war.

Twenty-five former officers were drawing pension, the senior being former PC 38 R. McDonald, who had joined in December 1864 and was superannuated in 1887, and the junior being former PC 60 B. Hackett, who had been pensioned in 1915.

After the war it was realised that police pay and working standards were low when compared to other occupations, and strikes by police had taken place in London and Liverpool, so, as a result of the unrest, the Desborough Committee was set up to look into the matter of pay, pensions and conditions of service. Their findings meant that, for the first time, there would be national rates of pay and a standard code of discipline. New pay scales, brought into effect in this county on 10th. October 1919 meant that Constables, with starting pay of three pounds, ten shillings per week, reached four pounds after ten years service, with extra discretionary increments of two shillings and six pence, for good conduct and efficiency, at seventeen years and twenty two years, to a maximum of four pounds, fifteen shillings. Sergeants pay began at five pounds weekly, rising by half-crown increments, to five pounds, twelve shillings and six pence. Superintendents started at three hundred and fifty pounds per annum, rising annually by fifteen pounds, to a maximum four hundred and twenty-five pounds after five years, plus an allowance for the horse. The Deputy Chief Constable received an extra twenty pounds per annum, and the Chief Constable started at five hundred and fifty pounds, with ten pound annual increments to six hundred and fifty pounds. Twelve days Annual Leave, in addition to the weekly rest day, were also granted but this was not effective until 1920. The rent allowance payable to those Superintendents who did not occupy police property was to be twenty-five pounds per annum in lieu of rent and rates, and married Sergeants and Constables were to have a rent and rates-free house or a discretionary payment of five shillings per week, with the same amount payable to unmarried men as Lodging Allowance. All ranks were to receive two shillings per month for oil, one shilling and six pence weekly for boots, and one and a half pence per mile bicycle allowance when used for special, approved purposes. Six pence per meal was allowed for the maintenance of prisoners. A Police Federation for England and Wales came into being, allowing all ranks to express views on welfare and efficiency, via their Branch Board, and ultimately to the Home Secretary. The first meeting of the Herefordshire Branch Boards took place at the Shire Hall on the 28th. October 1919. When put together these measures meant that officers began to feel like valued members of the community, and that they were rewarded accordingly, enjoying the confidence and respect of most of the population they served.

Domestic changes in Herefordshire at the same time saw the retirement on 1st November 1919, of the Deputy Chief Constable, F.W. Dallow, who had served the Constabulary for sixty years, possibly a national record.

Francis Worthington Dallow was born in Church Lench, Worcestershire, c.1839. He was appointed on 16th. September 1859, and served in Hereford, Abbeydore, Bromyard, Abbeydore, Leominster Divisions. Whilst serving in Ledbury Division he was promoted to Sergeant in 1864, and moved to Headquarters in 1866. Promoted to Superintendent in 1876, he became Deputy Chief Constable on 1st. July 1898. This photograph, with his wife, Susan, whom he married in 1875, was taken during his brief retirement in Newport, Mon. He died on 28th. July 1923, his wife died ten days later.

Sergeant 36 L. Lewis, who had been assistant to Mr.

Dallow, was promoted Superintendent/Chief Clerk in his stead, and PC 60 T.B. Wheeler, who had been appointed to the Constabulary on Armistice Day, 1918, became Assistant Clerk.

A Police Pensions Act was passed in 1921, with a twenty-five years qualifying period, and amended provision was made for widows and dependent children. With the approval of the Home Secretary in a letter dated October 1921, a bicycle allowance of five pounds per year was paid to Sergeants in charge of sub-divisions, in lieu of the three half-pence per mile which they had been receiving, but only where the bicycle was used for special purposes approved by the Chief Constable.

The retirement in 1921 of Superintendent T. Wright of Weobley, who had re-joined the Constabulary as PC 28, in October 1891, was seen as an opportune time to make Weobley into a section station in Leominster Division. This enlargement of the Division indicated the need for the first motor-car, and a Ford car, registration number CJ 4745, was provided for the use of Superintendent Charles Rooke, at Leominster, together with permission for a Constable to act as his driver, when needed. Superintendent Rooke had started his police career in 1883 and when he retired at the end of December 1921 his place at Leominster was taken by Superintendent J. Groves, who moved from Bromyard, which then became a section station in Ledbury Division. These changes were in line with the recommendations of the Geddes Committee which advised the Home Secretary to recommend that Police Authorities reduce their strengths by at least five per cent, by natural wastage, as part of a government cost-cutting exercise. By early 1923 the Divisional Superintendents at Hereford and Ledbury had also been provided with cars, in lieu of their annual horse allowance, leaving only the Superintendent at Ross with his horse and cart.

Superintendent Thomas Wright,

Thomas Wright was first appointed in 1884 as PC 8, and served in the Herefordshire Constabulary for five years, before resigning to join the Birmingham City Police. One year later he was back in Herefordshire as PC 28, later rising to the rank of Superintendent.

The end of 1921 and beginning of 1922 proved to be momentous in the life of the small hamlet of Cusop, part of Bredwardine section. A local solicitor, Major Herbert Rouse Armstrong, who practised in Hay, resided at Cusop with his wife and family, and after a series of events which have been well documented, he was arrested on suspicion of the attempted murder of a fellow solicitor in the town. Following further enquiries he was charged with the murder of his wife, Katharine, and was committed by the magistrates to appear at the Assize Court. Major Armstrong's trial at Hereford, where he was found guilty and sentenced to death, attracted enormous publicity. His appeal was dismissed, and he was hung at Gloucester in May 1922

Superintendent Albert Weaver
joined the Herefordshire Constabulary on 1st. December 1894, and was promoted to Superintendent in 1911, becoming Deputy Chief Constable in November 1919.
He was involved with the enquiries into the Armstrong murder, along with officers from Scotland Yard, and received a commendation from the Director of Public Prosecutions.
He was a native of Herefordshire, and was still a serving officer at the time of his death on 7th. September 1934.

Captain Stanhope's ill-health forced his retirement on 30th. September 1923 and the occasion was marked by a gathering of all ranks at Hereford to make a presentation to Captain and Mrs Stanhope. On behalf of the officers and constables the Deputy Chief Constable, Superintendent A. Weaver, presented a gold-mounted fountain pen to Mrs Stanhope, and a solid gold cigarette case, with an engraved family crest, to the retiring Chief Constable. In passing on the best wishes of all concerned Superintendent Weaver mentioned the respect and esteem in which Captain and Mrs. Stanhope were held, and went on to say that the Chief Constable 'had always tempered discipline with kindness', and they were deeply sorry to lose him. He expressed regret at the circumstances of Captain Stanhope's retirement and hoped he would recover his good health.

HEREFORDSHIRE CONSTABULARY, 1923-1929

Horace Frederick Moncrieff Munro,
Chief Constable of Herefordshire, 1923 – 1929

H.F.M. Munro was born in 1884 in Edinburgh, Scotland, and was educated at the Royal High School in that city, followed by Edinburgh University, where he gained a Master of Arts degree in 1906.

After a short teaching career, during which he was commissioned as a 2nd. Lieutenant in the Army Service Corps Special Reserve, he became a cadet officer in the Royal Irish Constabulary in 1909. He was posted to County Tyrone in 1910, taking charge of six stations and 40 men. Secondment to the War Office followed in November 1914, and he was promoted to Captain in the Army Service Corps in 1915. After service in England and France he was demobilised in 1919, to resume his career in the Royal Irish Constabulary. He served at Roscommon, Ennis, West Clare, County Monaghan and Kerry, where he was in charge of over 500 men. Following the setting up of the Irish Free State Captain Munro was appointed to the Irish Office. He married early in 1923, and, after his appointment as Chief Constable, he and his wife, Eleanor Anne, resided in Hereford, where three of their four children were born. He was a recipient of the Kings Police Medal, and was honoured with the OBE in 1943. After a very active life Captain Munro died in 1974, in his ninety-first year.

Captain Munro was chosen to become the Chief Constable of Herefordshire from a short list of eight, selected from about one hundred applicants, who included Mr. Thomas Rawson, at that time in charge of Hereford City Police. Chief Constable Munro was destined to remain as Chief Constable for the shortest time of the five holders of the post, but, in the time that he had, he made an impact on the police service in the county, and his regard for the welfare of his men, coupled with his attitude of fair discipline, ensured that he, in turn, was held in high regard.

Horse-drawn vehicles were common but use of motor vehicles was increasing, and the need to control traffic was growing. In May 1923 a national conference of representatives from the Metropolitan, County, City and Borough Police Forces took place, and the Secretary of the Automobile Association subsequently issued a pamphlet on the standardisation of signals, to be used by police officers controlling traffic, and by drivers of motor cars and other types of transport. It was believed that the observance of the suggested uniform code of signals, would not only minimise the risk of accidents, but would be of significant assistance to the public and also to the police. The pamphlet described the suggested signals in text, illustrations and photographs, and was issued to the police service and other interested bodies, with a recommendation that the contents be adopted.

The replacement of the railway tunnel between Malvern and Ledbury brought large numbers of workers to that part of Herefordshire. Extra police cover was needed, and in December 1923 PC 19 A.C.J. Edwards (known as 'Tiny' because of his large stature) moved from Kington to Colwall and remained there until the tunnel was completed in 1926.

Early in 1924 the Chief Constable issued new instructions about the form which written reports should take. He stressed that relevant facts should be made clear, in plain language, and reports should begin with 'I beg to report', and end with name, rank and number, with a margin of one and a half inches on the left. The old form of address, 'I am, Sir, your obedient servant,' was no longer to be used.

One sign of progress and the use of new aids was the arrangement made in April 1925 for the national broadcasting of urgent messages by the BBC. Locally, progress was slow in the field of mobility for beat officers. A General Order, issued in 1925, clarified the position regarding the use of an officer's own pedal-cycle, or motor-cycle. A rate of one and a half pence per mile was approved, payable to officers using private cycles to respond to emergencies, providing such use resulted in benefit to the public. Two pence per mile was payable if a motor-cycle was used, and the Order gave an example of how money could be saved, to the public good, by using a side-car. 'The officer at Leintwardine conveys a prisoner from Wigmore to Bucknell railway station, a distance of six miles. He then leaves his motor-cycle combination at the railway station, ready for his own return to Leintwardine, after conveying the prisoner by train. The normal amount payable for the same journey using a motor-car would be nine shillings, but by using the motor cycle the officer would claim only one shilling for the journey with a passenger (prisoner), and eight pence for his own return journey'. In addition, cycle allowance would be paid for certain recurring duties, such as attendance at Headquarters, courts and inquests. If an alternative form of transport was available the estimated cost of that should be shown on the claim, and the lower amount would be paid. Superintendents were now authorised to permit the use of cycles on normal patrol duty, but no allowance would be payable. After sixty-eight years the officer on patrol was permitted, at last, to use his bicycle! Being very careful not to make life too easy, in August of that year the Standing Joint Committee made it clear that the use of private motor-cars on duty was prohibited, but three pence per mile would be payable for private motor-cycle combinations used for necessary purposes, and carrying a passenger.

In June 1925 Captain Munro reported that during the previous quarter three hundred and fifteen persons had been brought before the Justices, thirty-three indictable offences were reported, and eight persons had been sent to gaol. One hundred and seventy two people had been fined, and three had been committed for trial. The Police, as Food and Drugs Inspectors, had taken samples, for checking, of milk, butter, margarine, lard, vinegar, white pepper, arrowroot, ground ginger, demerara sugar, tea and coffee, in various parts of the county, and all were found to be genuine. A total estimate of nearly six and a half thousand pounds for all police expenses for the forthcoming quarter, included:-

Salaries, Pay and Allowances,	£5,123
Three Reservists on Hop-picking Duty	£71
Boots	£55
Clothing and Accoutrements	£469
Postage, Telegrams & Telephone	£60
Repairs, Rents, Rates and Taxes	£300

More time was now available for recreation, and participation in sporting activities was encouraged by the Chief Constable, who often turned out for the Constabulary football team. During his university days Captain Munro had been awarded an Association Football 'Blue' and gained eighteen 'A' team cricket colours. He had also been a member of the University 'Eight' in the inter-university shooting competition in 1906, and continued his sporting interests into retirement, playing team cricket in Ayrshire until he was in his seventies.

COUNTY POLICE FOOTBALL TEAM, 1925

Back row, L. to R: T.A. Barwell, C.R. Moody, W.J. Lines, A. Moss, J. Chance, J. Edge, E.S. Edwards, T.B. Wheeler, R. Edwards.

Seated: E. Jarrett, H.F.M. Munro, S.G. Whittaker, A.F. Rock, A.H. Moss.

A letter from Sir Leonard Dunning, His Majesty's Inspector of Constabulary, to the Standing Joint Committee, was received in March 1925 suggesting that there should be a definite policy on housing the members of the Constabulary. Other than those housed in the established police stations, or other county property, fifty-six houses were rented and most were considered to be 'bad in themselves' , or 'unsuitably placed for the purpose of duty', or could put the police authority in a difficult position should the owner require repossession. Three married men were living in furnished apartments because no house could be found for them. Houses at Bredenbury, Wellington, Ledbury, Ross, Leominster, Ashperton and St. Weonards needed to be replaced because of their condition, and those at Kingstone, Kingsthorne, Tarrington, Whitchurch, Bredwardine, Staunton-on-Wye and Leysters were thought to be in the wrong position for the purposes of duty. Notice to quit the houses at Orleton, Leintwardine, Pontrilas and Weobley meant that those properties must be replaced. Sir Leonard pointed out that a 'proper house' would give 'the Constable stationed in a village far greater influence for good than he can exercise when his cottage is notably amongst the worst'. He went on to suggest that the eight hundred pounds annually spent on rents, would go a long way to paying the interest on a loan to initiate a housing scheme. The police station-house at Wigmore was again causing problems, and a furnace needed to be replaced at a cost of two pounds, twelve shillings and six pence.

The County Treasurer reported, at the end of 1925, that one thousand pounds had been allocated to housing, and some changes took place almost immediately, when the officer from Kingstone was moved to a council house at Much Dewchurch, and the house at Staunton-on-Wye was given up, in favour of one situated on the main road at Handmore Cross. New tenancies for better class cottages were agreed, where possible, and in 1926 the first police authority-owned house was purchased at Leintwardine, for the sum of two hundred and five pounds.

A plan of 'Alarm and Pursuit' to be put into action in cases of serious crime, when the offenders tried to escape, was drawn up in December 1925, detailing the forms of warning to be used and the sequence of how the alert would be passed from station to station. It involved an arrangement for the communication of information, and action in holding key 'fixed points'. The alarms were split into three categories:

1. General Police Alarm, when the whole Force would be called out.
2. Police Warning, when only sections would be called out.
3. Practice Alarm, when no crime had been committed, but to test the scheme.

A list of the locations of the 'fixed points' to be set up was included, together with instructions on what action should be taken:

Prepare to block the road with whatever means available.

Make enquiries and detain suspects.

Special emphasis was placed on the importance of keeping in touch with the 'fixed points'.

The Divisional Headquarters in Burgess Street, Leominster had, for some time, been lacking in facilities, operating mainly from the Superintendent's house, the cells at the rear, and the court witnesses waiting room being utilised as an office for the Superintendent. A vacant Savings Bank building next door to the Superintendent's house became available, and in October 1926 it was taken on a 21 year lease at forty pounds per annum. Clerical cover, when needed by the Superintendent, was provided by PC 53 F.J. Little.

The former Savings Bank building in Leominster which became the Police Station in 1926, and was still in use in the 1950's when this photograph of Sergeant 56 L.A. Workman, the Clerk, was taken.
The building to the left of the Police Station was originally the Superintendent's house, taken over as Divisional Headquarters, and later also included the CID office.

The Geddes Report recommendations of 1922 were enacted and a general re-organisation by Captain Munro, spread over several years, streamlined the force. Reductions by natural wastage, reduced the strength from eighty-six men to eighty-four, bringing the number of Superintendents down to two. One of the first General Orders of the new Chief Constable in October 1923 had been to clarify the designation of the Divisions, which were to be known as Hereford, Ledbury, Ross and Leominster Divisions. Petty Sessional Divisions within these Constabulary Divisions would be known as Sections.

In 1925 the Ledbury Superintendent was transferred to Leominster, and Ledbury then became a section station in Ross Division, thus reducing the number of Divisions to three. The Superintendent's horse allowance was dispensed with in 1925, as all Superintendents by then had the use of a Divisional car, with Constables designated to act as drivers when required. PC 24 M.A. Barter moved to Ross for this purpose, and PC 49 H.C. Bowery undertook the duties at Leominster. The Superintendent at Hereford had the services of PC 45 J.R. Cole as driver, and the Chief Constable carried out his supervisory duties using his own motor-cycle combination. Two Inspector posts were created, and the first officer to be promoted was Sergeant 25 Joshua Edge who became Inspector at Leominster in 1928. At the end of the same year Superintendent W.J. Hutchinson, who had been the Chief Clerk at Hereford, and had moved to Ross on the retirement of Superintendent J. Broad in 1927, left Ross to become Chief Constable of Worcester City. As the final step in the reduction of the number of Superintendents Ross then became a section station, with an Inspector in charge, under the supervision of the Hereford Superintendent. The Sergeant promoted to Inspector at Ross was Henry W. Williams, who had joined the Constabulary as PC 42 in January 1906.

The departure of Superintendent Hutchinson from Hereford in 1927 had left the newly promoted Sergeant/Clerk 60 T.B. Wheeler to run the office, assisted by a Junior Clerk, the forerunner of a Police Cadet, named Kenneth Charles Weaver, who later became PC 17 and eventually rose to the rank of Superintendent, and Deputy Chief Constable, as had his father, Albert Weaver, before him. The last two Sergeants in charge of single rural beats, Sergeant 28 E.D.H. Walters of Whitestone and Sergeant 20 S.G. Whittaker of Colwall, moved to Harewood End and Wigmore, and the two beats which they vacated were taken over by PC 65 G. Williams, who moved from Bromyard to Whitestone and PC 48 J.J. White, who moved from Kington to Colwall. Thereafter all rural beats were manned by Constables, and Sergeants were in charge of Section Stations.

The integrity and forthrightness of Captain Munro can be judged from his reply to someone who had offered a gratuity to a Constable. He wrote that he felt very sorry that the individual should have thought it necessary to offer such a gratuity, as, for a long time the efforts of the Police had been directed towards raising the status of the Force, and the offer of such a gratuity would put a man into a very difficult position in deciding whether to sink his pride in the Service and accept a private benefit, or to uphold the prestige of the Service. The Chief Constable went on to point out that no officer could accept a gratuity without applying for the permission of the Chief Constable, which permission he would give if asked for, but it would affect his opinion of the applicant, to the applicant's detriment.

In December 1926 the Treasurer had reported that there were at that time fifty-three pensioners, made up of thirty-nine former police officers, seven widows and seven dependent children. At a Standing Joint Committee meeting in October 1928 the Chief Constable reported that pensions for the ensuing quarter would amount to one thousand six hundred and thirty-eight pounds, and the running costs of the Police would be five thousand, nine hundred and fifty-four pounds. An unspecified number of helmets and caps were to be supplied by Hobsons at a cost of more than thirty-eight pounds, and articles of clothing from Compton would cost four hundred and seventy eight pounds.

Once again Wigmore was in the news, and plans were afoot to upgrade the inadequate living accommodation, by provision of an extra living-room and a scullery, improved sanitary arrangements, and complete separation from the prisoner's cells, at a cost of three hundred and sixty pounds.

From the beginning of the Constabulary new recruits had received a very short course of training, usually not more than two weeks at Headquarters, learning partly by example from a parent constable, who would show him how to carry out his duties, with further instruction being given by Superintendents at Divisional or Sectional parades, or pay parades. By the mid-twenties the larger forces had established their own training schools, and the Standing Joint Committee in Herefordshire was pleased to follow the advice of His Majesty's Inspector and arrangements were made by the Chief Constable, that all recruits

PC 34 D. Grigg as a new recruit.

would, in future receive three months formal training, at an initial cost of fifty shillings per recruit. The first officer to go for instruction at a training school was PC 34 D. Grigg, who went to the Cardiff City Police Training School in July 1927, and shortly afterwards PCs 45 G. Christopher, 30 E. E. Bendall and 69 T. Craig went to the Birmingham City Police Training School. Some later trainees went to the Swansea City School.

West Sussex County Council had submitted a plan to the Herefordshire Standing Joint Committee, which met with their approval, to the effect that too much police time was being taken up in traffic management, which was not considered to be primarily police duty. They intended to ask the Home Secretary whether a subsidiary force, under the control of the police, could be set up, but on lower pay rates than police officers, and might provide a useful source of recruitment. West Sussex County Council considered that in the absence of such a scheme more police officers would be required, 'at a serious cost to the rate-payers'. The suggested organised force did not materialise, although in Herefordshire RAC and AA Scouts began to be used for occasional traffic control, mainly in Ledbury, Leominster and Ross.

The Constabulary Headquarters at Hereford, and all Divisional Headquarters had telephones installed by 1927, and a start had been made on connecting other stations, but because of the cost of an isolated installation, the scheme was dependent on the availability of other telephones in the area. Nine out-stations had telephones installed, at Much Marcle, Kingsland, Peterchurch, Pontrilas, Whitchurch, Bodenham, St. Weonards and Cradley, but this still left more than thirty out-stations out of reach by telephone. A General Order in June 1927 instructed that an Occurrence Book would be kept at all stations, which was to be regarded as a station record, not a personal record, and would remain there if a move occurred. Entries were to be full enough to ascertain all facts, with particular attention to time and place, and events in the proper order. A list of events to be recorded included everything from accidents to Diseases of Animals, robberies to reports of 'sick and unfit for duty', to name but a few.

Instructions were issued in 1928 as to the correct form of salute to be given when meeting superiors, and the list of who should receive such salutation included Royalty, the Lord Lieutenant, H.M. Judges, all members of the Standing Joint Committee, Magistrates, the Clerk of the Peace, and senior officers of other Police Forces. Details of what should occur if marching, or wearing civilian clothes were not forgotten, even the distance that one should stand in front of a superior officer when addressing him was specified.

In December 1927 the appointment of Mr. Freeman Newton as Chief Constable of Hereford City Police, appeared to have little bearing on the County Constabulary at the time, but the future was to prove otherwise. Chief Constable Munro left Herefordshire at the end of January 1929 to return to his native Scotland, as Chief Constable of Ayrshire, with the satisfaction of knowing that all the organisational changes which he had made were proving to be effective. His place in Herefordshire was taken by Mr. Freeman Newton, who began his dual role as Chief Constable of Herefordshire Constabulary and of Hereford City Police.

A Conference of senior officers of several Police Forces was held in Hereford in 1926. Pictured above, outside the West front of Hereford Cathedral, are the delegates, including Captain H.F.M. Munro and Superintendent A. Weaver. (front row, fifth from right and second from right respectively).

HEREFORDSHIRE CONSTABULARY, 1929-1958

Freeman Newton,
Chief Constable of Herefordshire, 1929 – 1958

Mr. Freeman Newton was born in London in 1891 and after finishing his education at London University he took up duties as an Assistant Superintendent with the Indian (Imperial) Police. Whilst based in Mandalay, Burma his aptitude, dedication and knowledge of native languages quickly brought promotion, and by 1917 he was a District Superintendent commanding 500 officers, in an area with a population of half a million. Unfortunately the climate in Burma had a debilitating effect on the health of Mrs Newton, and the decision was made to return to her native Wales.

Mr. Newton was appointed Chief Constable of Hereford City Police in late 1927, and in early 1929 he took on the added responsibility of the post of Chief Constable of the County Constabulary. He organised the merger of the two forces of which he had charge, in 1947, and continued in the post until his retirement in 1958. In 1941 Mr. Newton was awarded the King's Police and Fire Services Medal, and was honoured with the OBE in 1954.

His retirement years were spent in Hereford, where he remained a familiar figure until his death in 1976, aged 84 years.

When Mr. Freeman Newton began his duties with the County Constabulary he had the advantage of having been in the area for just over a year, and therefore had some familiarity with the city and county. His residence was De Lacy House, Gaol Street, close to the city police station, where he continued to live for about twenty years.

THE PRE-WAR PERIOD, 1929 – 1939.

The appointment of new officers to maintain the establishment of eighty four was controlled by the Home Office under the economy measures already imposed by the Geddes Report and approval had to be obtained before any appointments could be made to fill the four vacancies which existed in 1929. More economy measures, which came into effect on 1st.October 1931, meant that new entrants actually began with a lower rate of pay, but by regular increments eventually met the established standard rate.

The Herefordshire Constabulary Benevolent Association was formed on the 1st. April 1930, funded by weekly subscription from members, augmented by other fund-raising social activities. Its aims were to assist serving members of the Constabulary if in need, and to supplement the pensions of widows. The committee was led by the Chief Constable, with the Deputy Chief Constable, A. Weaver, Superintendent G.T. Brierley, Sergeant 28 E.D.H. Walters, Sergeant 80 L.J. Jones, PC 27 E.S. Edwards, PC 49 H.C. Bowery, PC 37 A.E. Matthews, and PC 69 T. Craig as the first committee members, with Sergeant 60 T.B. Wheeler acting as Secretary and Treasurer.

The labour training camps which had been set up at Wigmore and Shobdon, to provide three monthly forestry courses for groups of three hundred and fifty trainees from the depressed areas of Lancashire and South Wales, required extra supervision and once again PC 19 A.C.J. (Tiny) Edwards was moved into the area from Ross, in order to handle the situation, until the camps were finally closed in 1936. Following the retirement of PC 43 A.G. Tompkins from Lyonshall in June 1930, the beat which he had covered was divided between the neighbouring beats of Eardisley and Pembridge, and an extra officer was posted to Kington. Two deaths which are worthy of mention occurred during that year, the first, in October, was of a serving officer, PC 26 J.H. Francis, of Upton Bishop, at the age of forty-eight, who, at six feet tall and twenty-six stone was reputed to be one of the heaviest policemen in the land. The second death, in Scotland, was that of Robert McDonald, aged eighty-six years, who had been a Herefordshire pensioner for forty-three years.

As a consequence of the implementation of the Road Traffic Act, of 1930, mobile patrols were set up within the county, and in February 1931 three Sunbeam motor-cycles and one motor-cycle combination were purchased, and three officers, PC 67 F.J. Griffin, PC 45 G. Christopher and PC 30 E.E. Bendall, were based in the Hereford Division and together with PC 65 G. Williams, who was based at Leominster, became the mobile patrol. At the end of 1933, after two years of constant use the motor-cycles had almost reached the end of their useful life, and it was decided to replace them with two Morris ten horse-power cars, using the motor-cycles as part payment. This change released two officers for normal duties and PC 45 G. Christopher was posted to Ledbury, and PC 30 E.E. Bendall moved to Ross. The two officers who had acted as Superintendent's drivers, PC 47 W.H. Franzen, who was a qualified motor-mechanic, at Hereford, and PC 49 H.C. Bowery, at Leominster, acted as observers when required, in order that speeds could be checked and corroborative evidence given, if needed.

Another responsibility for all officers was their appointment, by the Local Authority in October 1932, as Inspectors under the Diseases of Animals Acts. These duties, which fell mainly onto the officers in rural areas, included checking the Movement of Animals Register, which all farmers were required to keep, distributing, collecting and recording Forms A, B, C and D covering sheep-dipping, and visiting some farms to ensure that the dipping was correctly carried out. The supervision of the destruction, usually by burning, of animals suffering from Anthrax, and the restriction of entry to premises by unauthorised persons, when Foot and Mouth Disease broke out, the issuing of Movement Licences, particularly when cases of Swine Fever occurred, and duty at Cattle Markets throughout the county were all included as duties under the Act.

In celebration of his Silver Jubilee, in July 1935, King George the Fifth carried out a review of all police forces in Hyde Park, London, and the officers chosen to represent Herefordshire were Sergeant 6 A. Lewis, PC 72 T. Rees, PC 27 E.S. Edwards, PC 1 C.F. Harris, PC 61 E.C. Wills, PC 9 A.R.Smith, PC 14 A. Moss, and PC 67 F.J. Griffin. Medals in celebration of the same event were awarded to the Chief Constable, Superintendent Brierley, Superintendent J. Edge, Inspector S.G. Whittaker, Sergeant 28 E.D.H. Walters, Sergeant 60 T.B. Wheeler and PC 27 E.S. Edwards.

Housing was becoming an ever more urgent issue, as standards of living, generally, began to rise, and the level of police accommodation and amenities failed to keep pace. In fact, in 1929, the Medical Officer of Health condemned the police cottage at Longtown as 'unfit for human habitation', and the tenancy of another cottage in the village had to be quickly obtained. At about the same time the rented cottage at Walford was purchased for three hundred and twenty-five pounds, and two years later two more rented cottages, at The Downs, Bromyard, and at Dilwyn were purchased, followed by the cottage at Wellington which cost the Authority two hundred and twenty pounds in 1932. Plans were in hand for the erection of a new house to be occupied by the Sergeant at Kington, which, combined with alterations to the court-room, would cost just over one thousand pounds.

PC 34 D. Grigg, outside the Police Station at St. Weonards, which was purchased for £300 in 1933.

After attention had been drawn to the fact that the annual rent bill stood at over one thousand pounds the Standing Joint Committee came to the conclusion that it would be economical, and would prove more efficient, if a scheme was embarked upon whereby the police authority became the owners of all the houses in the rural areas. The purchasing programme went ahead, and by December 1933 the police authority owned twenty houses, for the upkeep of which it was now responsible, and it was still paying rent on forty-eight others.

Plots of land were purchased, and plans drawn up for a series of similar houses which were built between 1934 and 1939. The first of these to be occupied, by PC 8 J. Bayliss, was the police station at Stretton Sugwas, at a cost of under six hundred pounds. The houses at Llangarron, Longtown, Orleton, Allensmore and Bringsty, Much Marcle and Leysters, were all completed by 1939, with the last one being the police station at Burley Gate, which was delayed because of problems with the water supply, but was finally occupied in December 1939 by PC 76 H.E.J. Penry. The problems with the water supply at the house were an on-going saga which continued until mains water was laid there in the late-1960's. A new house for the Inspector at Ross replaced one which had been described as defective, through dampness in the walls, insufficient window space and lack of ventilation in the bedrooms, and the need for redecoration throughout. Sites had also been purchased for four other houses, and for a new police station at Ledbury, but when further building had to cease, shortly after the outbreak of war in 1939, the sites were fenced off, and remained so until after the war ended.

The allowances to be paid for travelling were reviewed again in 1935, and those for the use of private vehicles on public service, were fixed as follows: pedal cycles, one penny per mile; motor-cycles, with or without sidecar, two pence per mile; tri-cars and four-wheeled cars, to eight horse-power, three pence per mile; larger horse-power vehicles, three and a half pence, or four pence per mile. The Chief Constable emphasised, in an Order in February 1935, that it should be clearly understood that no journey should be undertaken by car unless on a matter of urgency, and the use of a motor-vehicle for ordinary patrol duties would not, under any circumstances, be allowed. However, the need for more mobility, coupled with the necessity to be able to respond to situations, was becoming more evident, and the mobile section was expanded in 1936, when two more cars were purchased, a ten horse-power Morris, and a nine horse-power Singer, both to operate in the Hereford Division, with PC 55 D.H. Roberts and PC 18 F.G. Stephens as drivers. These two cars had a short life, as, in July 1937 the four vehicles then in use were replaced by two ten horse-power Morris cars, registration numbers, ACJ 282 and ACJ 283, and two fourteen horse-power Rover cars, registration numbers, ACJ 280 and ACJ 281, which could be used as vehicles to test the speed of other road users. The intention was that these vehicles would be used until 1st. January 1939, and thereafter vehicles would be changed annually. Plans were in hand for the provision of garages, to be built at the rear of the Shire Hall, and by 1939 the mobile patrol section was incorporated into Headquarters Division, with PC 65 G. Williams stationed at Leominster, and three officers at Hereford, PC 18 F.G. Stephens, PC 60 D.C. Stacey and PC 12 F.A. Jackson.

The Chief Constable made strong representation to the Standing Joint Committee in 1937, recommending an increase of four in the strength, a Sergeant and a Constable at Headquarters, and two Constables to be stationed at Rotherwas and Callow. He stated that this was due to the ever increasing duties and responsibilities of the police, and in line with statistical surveys made by the Home Office, the committee agreed to the suggestion, subject to Home Office approval. Earlier that year the Chief Clerk, T.B. Wheeler, had been promoted to the rank of Inspector, and with the extra Constable at Headquarters, it was decided that the position of Junior Clerk would be dispensed with.

The need for a Criminal Investigation Department had been stressed by His Majesty's Inspector of Constabulary, and PC 20 F.M. Bayley attended an eight week CID course at Wakefield, early in 1938, following Sergeant 17 K.C. Weaver who had attended a photographic course the previous year. In December 1938 PC Bayley moved from Much Marcle to Hereford, where he was to undertake detective duties, prior to the formation of the new CID department, which took place on 1st. May 1939.

Increased administration meant that office accommodation was becoming cramped in the four rooms of the Headquarters building, erected in 1898 at the Shire Hall, and it was decided that this building would in future serve as the Hereford Divisional Headquarters, and other premises would be sought for County Headquarters. In June 1939 a fourteen year lease was agreed, on numbers 1, and 1a, St. John Street, Hereford, at a cost of one hundred pounds per annum, exclusive of rates. The building had to be furnished and three telephones, with five extensions, were installed to cater for the communication needs of the Headquarters and administrative staff, as well as the CID and mobile section, all of whom were in place by the 19th. September 1939. A series of promotions in the Administrative department saw Inspector T.B. Wheeler promoted to Chief Inspector, and Sergeant 17 K.C. Weaver made Inspector. PC 67 F.J. Griffin left the mobile section to take a new administrative post at Divisional Headquarters, and two posts of Sergeant/ Clerk, advertised nationally, were filled by C. Foster who came from the Doncaster Borough Police, as Sergeant 17 at Headquarters, and C.W. Wallin, from the West Riding Constabulary, who became Sergeant 85, at Leominster Divisional Headquarters.

Preparations for impending war were under way and regardless of the restrictions which there had been previously, concerning recruitment, all police forces were now being urged to increase their numbers. From April 1939 two officers were seconded for Air Raid Precaution duties; Inspector E.D.H. Walters, of Leominster, organised the preparations in north Herefordshire, and Sergeant 53 F.J. Little, of Ross, carried out the same duties for South Herefordshire. As a security measure, all members of the Constabulary were finger-printed, and the records were kept for future reference. The Chief Constable reported to the Standing Joint Committee in July that the Home Office were anxious that all police forces would be ready to pass on to a war footing without any delay, but he pointed out that even with the Constabulary up to the approved strength of ninety, plus the two who were seconded, there would be no provision in any of the county towns to allow for leave, or absence through sickness. The committee was reluctant to take any action which would put an increased charge on the County Rates, but eventually agreed to the Chief Constable's request that the Constabulary should be increased by one Chief Inspector, two Sergeants and nine Constables, making the proviso that the numbers should not increase beyond one hundred and one, without their prior approval.

'Show me the enemy!'
PC 82 H. Broadhead, during ARP training.

Life in rural Herefordshire continued normally, and in early September nine officers left their stations, in order to assist the resident officers of nine rural beats with the annual influx of casual labour which arrived in the county for the seven week hop-picking season, but, within a few days of their arrival the world was changed, when on 3rd. September, war was declared.

THE WAR PERIOD, 1939 – 1945.

The plans which had been prepared for such an emergency were put into action, and fortunately there was a delay, until at least 1st. December, before any serving officers who were already reservists, would have to leave the county for war service, and restrictions were put on others who might want to enlist. The Chief Constable now had to take charge of the First Police Reserve, the Special Constabulary, the Police War Reserve, the Air Raid Wardens, the Observer Corps, and took on other responsibilities such as Public Warning Systems, A.R.P. communications, and enforcing Street Lighting Restrictions, in addition to his normal police duties.

This three months lull, when, although the country was at war, there had fortunately been no invasion or air-raids, gave time for the First Reserve to be called for duty, and for auxiliaries to be enrolled. Provision had to be made for the protection of essential services, such as gas, water and electricity, and to ensure the safety of certain secret premises and installations.

Between the 1st. and 4th. of December 1939, at the end of the three months which had been allowed, eighteen colour reservists left Herefordshire to re-join their regiments:

PC 41 D.B. Webb Royal Artillery
PC 79 G.A. Fletcher K.S.L.I.

Sixteen to the Brigade of Guards:
PC 4 J. H. Amos
PC 82 H. Broadhead
PC 54 W.J. Evans
PC 81 D.A. Gibson
PC 52 G.W.H. Hill
PC 89 V.A. Johanssen
PC 42 J.A. Kelly
PC 58 A. Mangham
PC 2 R.G. Plumbly
PC 69 L.L. Rees
PC 55 D.H. Roberts
PC 15 H.J. Scrine
PC 16 J.H. Stamp
PC 86 H.G. Venn
PC 25 W.R. Wakefield
PC 63 E. Wheatley

Between 1941 and 1943 three men volunteered for air-crew duties, and eight others were released for call-up to the forces:-

PC 21 J.S. Bourne
PC 83 C.A. Bullock
PC 88 C.E. Dominey
PC 90 A.L. Drennen
PC 39 R.J. Farmer
PC 70 G.H. Holman
PC 84 C.H. Lappage
DC 60 D.C. Stacey
Insp. K.C. Weaver
PC 87 W.J. Williams
PC 56 L.A. Workman

A stop on recruitment to the Constabulary came into effect in February 1940, shortly after the appointment of PC 92 J. Cook, and all officers were exempt from military service, for the time being. The Police and Firemen's (War Service) Act of 1939 ensured that those men who served in H.M. Forces would have their pay made up whilst serving. Officers who were due to retire on pension, were not allowed to do so, except by special permission of the Chief Constable, or on medical grounds, but application could be made for a pension, on the usual qualifying terms, in order to secure it for their eventual retirement. The officer's services would be retained, and an additional allowance was added to his pay, as a loss of earnings supplement.

During the preparations for war twenty-five former policemen had volunteered to

return to full-time service, if called upon, to serve in the First Police Reserve, and by November 1939 eleven of them were back on duty.
The eleven, who were allocated collar numbers 101 to 111 were:

101 E. Everett, (Herefordshire Constabulary), worked Fownhope beat.
102 P.J. Morrisey, (Royal Irish Constabulary), based at Bromyard.
103 J. Whittaker, (West Riding Constabulary), based at Kington.
104 T.A.Barwell, (Herefordshire Constabulary), based at Bodenham.
105 T. Probert, (Worcestershire Constabulary), based at Weobley.
106 E.Jarrett, (Herefordshire Constabulary), based at Eardisley.
107 H.W. Williams, (Herefordshire Constabulary), based at Ross, (Sergeant).
108 W.J.Brown, (Herefordshire Constabulary), based at Hereford and Clifford.
109 W.J. Griffin, (Herefordshire Constabulary) based at Bromyard.
110 O.C. Jones, (Cheshire Constabulary), based at Holme Lacy, (Sergeant).
111 L.A. Cullen, (Monmouthshire Constabulary), based at Lyonshall and Leominster.

FPR Constable 102 P.J. Morrisey resigned through ill-health in June 1941, to be replaced by FPR Sergeant 102 W.C. Gwynn, and FPRC 111 L.A. Cullen resigned on medical grounds in February 1942, and was not replaced.

The review of man-power in 1943, which reduced overall police coverage, allowed six First Police Reservists to resign on age or medical grounds, and of the remaining four FPR Constable E. Everett left in 1944, and at the end of the war two of the three remaining resigned. First Police Reserve Sergeant 102 W.C. Gwynn continued to serve at Bromyard, until he was posted to Dilwyn in August 1946, and resigned on 31st. December 1948 when the First Police Reserve was finally disbanded.

Security was of prime importance and in July 1940 the Criminal Investigation Department was increased by the transfer of PC 60 D.C. Stacey, as Detective Constable, and the promotion of DC 20 F. M. Bayley to Detective Sergeant. A Ford ten horse-power car was made available for their use. In August Chief Inspector T.B. Wheeler was made Personal Assistant to the Chief Constable to assist with the many extra war-time duties, and the general increase in administration tasks initiated more moves to cover the various aspects.

The first two CID officers in the county. L. to R: DC 60 D.C. Stacey and Det. Sgt. 20 F.M. Bayley

A second vital source of filling vacancies was provided by the use of War Reserve Constables. These were men over thirty years of age, mainly selected from the Special Constabulary, of adequate medical and educational qualifications, who worked alongside regular officers carrying out full police duties. Later in the war they became interchangeable with their regular counterparts, and occupied police housing where it became available, after an officer had joined the armed forces and his family moved out, often to stay with relatives.

The first two War Reserve Constables to be appointed were 201 G. Baynham and

202 F.G. Irish at Ross, and by the end of 1940 twenty men were spread throughout the county – twelve of them in the market towns, and WRPC 218 E. Patrick at Canon Pyon and WRPC 214 E.S. Cooke at Callow, working their beats single-handed. Four of the other officers assisted the regular officers at Abbeydore, Colwall, Whitchurch and Pontrilas, and two were attached to Wigmore section in order to protect the Elan Valley – Birmingham water pipe-line at vulnerable spots in the county.

WRPC 218 E. Patrick

The National Service Act of 1941 allowed willing conscripts to serve in the police, as an alternative to the armed forces, provided they were medically fit and had been vetted as being suitable. This allowed thirteen more War Reserves to be added, and when recruitment finally ceased in 1942 they numbered thirty-four. Following the review of man-power in 1943, seven War Reserves were released and directed by the Ministry of Labour into other essential work, and in 1944 War Reserve Constable 230 R. W. Tanner, of Headquarters, Mobile Section, enlisted in the army, one other officer resigned and five more were drafted into civilian war-work. At the end of the war eighteen men were released into civilian life, nine of them in 1945, and nine others in 1946. Three who were released, S.C. Mace, F.G. Irish and H. Deakin, later joined as regulars in 1947, the year which saw the end of the War Reserve when WRPC 207 A. Hicks was released from his duties at Bromyard, and War Reserve Constable 220 F. Arrowsmith became PC 93.

The forty-four War Reserves who served for varying lengths of time, and their colleagues of the First Police Reserve, provided essential cover for the men who had gone to the services, and a reliable support for the regular officers who remained behind.

Another auxiliary section whose members proved themselves to be invaluable was the Women's Auxiliary Police Corps. Twenty-one ladies served for varying periods between May 1940 and December 1946, carrying out clerical, typing and switchboard duties, and later, took over driving duties. In December 1939 the Home Office had given permission for two female civilian clerks (later to be known as WAPC) to be employed, and the two appointed were Mrs. P. A. King and Mrs. B.A. Hill, who began their duties on 1st. May 1940, as typists to the Chief Constable and the Chief Clerk. In August they were joined by two telephonists, working an eight hour shift each, daily, and a year later four more recruits were added. In June 1942 six more WAPCs were recruited to take over driving duties and administration, replacing enlisted Constables. WAPC A.B. Dowse was promoted to the rank of Leading Auxiliary in 1943.

The Special Constabulary had been organised into an operational unit in May 1939, but at the beginning of hostilities training was not complete, and was speeded up so that within a comparatively short time all ranks were fully conversant with Anti-gas and First Aid duties, had received instruction in fundamental police duties, and were ready to gain experience by performing duties in company with regular officers. In the first year of the war the Specials numbered a total of six hundred and eight, of whom ninety-three were available for duty in urban areas, five hundred and seven in rural areas, four formed the staff at Headquarters, to deal with the organisational needs of such a large voluntary force, which was under the control of the Commander, Brigadier-General T.R.F. Bate, CMG, and four others became members of the Special Emergency Mobile Unit. Throughout the war all sections diligently undertook whatever duties were asked of them, performing normal police duties when required and dealing with the enforcement of lighting restrictions, traffic control, supervision of aliens, guarding vulnerable points, and helping to deal with the disruption caused by large military convoys passing through the county. The members of the Mobile Unit received special training in traffic and messenger duties, and the Unit could call upon other members from each of the ten sections in the county, so that their work supplemented the duties of the regular mobile section. In common with the other auxiliary sections the numbers of the Special Constabulary were cut, to about four hundred, by the end of the war.

War-time conditions made extra police coverage necessary in some areas, and three war-time stations, at Holme Lacy, Little Brampton, Madley, and Mordiford had telephones installed and notice-boards erected in 1940. At Leominster the two rented houses in Church Street, together with the third, adjoining house, were purchased for one thousand, three hundred and fifty pounds, and the Superintendent's house in Burgess Street became Divisional office accommodation.

The war affected the civilian population in many ways, but fortunately Herefordshire was spared the massive air attacks which were suffered in other parts of the country. After the horrendous air-raid on Coventry in November 1940, a contingent of officers of the Mutual Aid Detachment were sent from Herefordshire to assist the police in that shattered city. Mr. Newton later received a letter of thanks from the Chief Constable of Coventry for the assistance given to his officers, 'following the foul and disastrous air-raid'.

PC 47 W.H. Franzen, based at Hereford, was seconded in June 1942, to the Ministry of Home Security (Transport), based at Bristol, and the following month saw the Constabulary reach its highest number of serving officers, with seventy-four regulars, ten First Police Reserve, thirty-three War Reserves, thirteen WAPCs, and three seconded officers.

The 'D-day' preparations in southern England, required extra police presence in certain areas, and on 1st. May 1944, a detachment of four officers, War Reserve PC 201 G. Baynham, War Reserve PC 222 G.A. Warrender, PC 26 C.J. Andrews and PC 11 W.E. Thomas, went from Herefordshire to Southampton, where they remained for duty until 21st. July.

Two Police Officers died during the war,

Edward Wheatley, died in France on 30th. May 1940,
Donald C. Stacey, died in Canada on 15th. November 1942.

The end of the war in 1945 saw the speedy return of men from the armed forces. One officer had returned to duty in 1942, and of the twenty-six remaining, twenty had returned to police duty before the end of the year, and two more returned in 1946. The last to return was PC 81 D.A. Gibson who was discharged from army hospital in 1947, to take up duties at Headquarters. Three men took up other occupations, two of them choosing to stay in the army, V.A. Johanssen with the Welsh Guards, and D.B. Webb, who retired from the army in 1958 with the rank of Lieutenant Colonel.

THE POST-WAR PERIOD, 1945 – 1958

The Chief Constable presented a long, and obviously well-considered report to the Standing Joint Committee in February 1945, preparing them for the reconstruction of the Police service after the end of the war, which was to be dealt with on a national basis by the Home Office, but needed consultation at local level. Mr. Newton mentioned in particular recruitment and training, but he also placed strong emphasis on housing, and the strength of the Constabulary. In November 1944 the Home Office had stressed the need for 'adequate housing' for police officers, and advocated the prompt acquisition of sites where it was perceived that there was a need.

The housing position in Herefordshire at that time was that the Police Authority owned thirty houses and rented thirty-one, and if all the married officers in the force returned to their duties there would be sixty-seven married men, without allowing for the twenty-three expected vacancies, of which at least half could be expected to be filled by married men – thus creating an immediate short-fall in housing. It could safely be assumed that twenty new houses would be needed, without taking into account the unsuitable housing which was already in use, and should be given up. This would make a likely requirement figure of around thirty houses, making a total of twenty-one building plots to be acquired, in addition to the ones purchased before the war.

The owners of three of the rented houses, at Peterchurch, Bishops Frome and Weston-under-Penyard, were anxious to regain possession of their properties, and fourteen others, including seven already owned by the Authority, were recognised as being in urgent need of replacement, with three of the rented properties, at Bosbury, Fownhope and Kingsland being top of the list. Some police-stations needed to be re-located, for example Abbeydore could be given up and moved to the more accessible Pontrilas, a move which had been suggested before the war. The unsuitable, rented house at Cusop which was occupied by a Sergeant, and the Constable's house at Bredwardine should both be dispensed with, and a new police station and court buildings, together with housing, erected at Clifford. The arrangement represented a saving of thirty pounds annual rental to Breconshire, for the infrequent use of the court at Hay. Other rural locations were mentioned, plus the need for at least three houses at Leominster, intended to replace the three in Church Street which had been purchased during the war.

It was stressed that the needs of the men must come first, but once again office accommodation was becoming a problem. The lease on the property at St. John Street still had eight years to run, but the building was described as being 'old and insubstantial', with 'walls that are bulging in places'. It was thought that the City Police would also be in need of new administrative accommodation, and whatever the future of the two forces might be, it was thought unlikely that the Secretary of State would give permission for two Police administrative buildings to be built in the same city, particularly when they had the same Chief Constable. It was advocated that one Headquarters building should be considered for the two Police Forces.

The Home Office recommended that the pre-war strength of the force, one hundred and two in 1939, should be used as the basis when assessing future needs of housing, and the numbers and disposition of the men. The Chief Constable suggested that an increase of six officers was applicable, involving an increase of four senior ranks, a decrease of four Constables, and, in view of the experience gained during the war years of their efficiency, loyalty and reliability, the appointment of six women should be considered, for clerical and driving duties, two of whom should be based at Leominster. The employment of women would also help to decrease costs, without sacrificing efficiency! The minimal size of the Criminal Investigation Department, was seen as being totally inadequate to deal with the increased incidence of crime, and the necessity to take advantage of the growth in both the use of scientific aids and advances in photography, therefore it was suggested that the department be increased to one Sergeant, and four Detective Constables, with two of the Constables being stationed at the Divisional offices at Leominster and Hereford.

After the war ended the Home Office endeavoured to rationalise the police service throughout the country, by dispensing with Borough police forces which served a population of less than 100,000, merging them with the police force of the county in which they were situated, and the Police Act of 1946, which implemented these changes, signalled the end for Hereford City Police. The latest date that these mergers could take place was 1st. April 1947, and at a meeting of the Standing Joint Committee, in June 1946, Mr. Newton put forward his proposals of how the amalgamation could be brought about, bearing in mind that he was already the Chief Constable of both forces. He thought that it would be necessary to alter the Divisional boundaries, and suggested that a City Division would need to be created, comprising the whole of the City of Hereford, together with Hereford Rural District, with a total area of over fifty thousand acres, and a population of just over forty-one thousand, and comprising eight urban and seven rural beats. The Northern Divisional Headquarters would remain at Leominster, and would continue with the five urban and nineteen rural beats already in existence. The newly constituted Southern Division, would almost equal the Northern Division in population and would consist of four urban beats and nineteen rural beats.

A recommendation had been made by the Home Office in January 1946 that a Traffic Department should be formed which should deal with:- road safety measures, review and investigate road accidents, the prosecution of traffic offences, compile maps and statistics of road events, organise the duties and training of officers engaged on motor patrol and advise all members of the Constabulary on methods of dealing with accidents which occurred, and suggest measures for preventing them. Other responsibilities of the new department would be the surveying of the positioning of pedestrian crossings and bus-stops, and parking places for the use of the public, together with liaison with the local Authority, and with the Education Authority regarding the teaching of road safety to school children. Dealing with this subject before the Standing Joint Committee, Mr Newton recommended that the man-power needed to fulfil these traffic functions would be one Inspector, two Sergeants and twenty Constables, assisted by two civilian clerks.

The Chief Constable pointed out that what he considered to be an extremely important branch of police work – the investigation of crime– had largely been neglected and he suggested that, because of the steady increase of reported crime and the increased mobility of the criminal, the strength of the Criminal Investigation Department of the new combined force should be one Detective Inspector, three Sergeants and ten constables, one of whom should be female. One Sergeant and two Constables should be stationed at each Divisional Headquarters.

With the amalgamation of the two forces the need for administrative officers at the single Headquarters could be reduced by four, and could, in future, be:- one Deputy Chief Constable, one Chief Inspector, one Inspector, one Sergeant, one Constable and two civilian clerks, together with four female telephonists. The fact that three buildings were in use in the City of Hereford as Headquarters and Divisional offices was again mentioned as being inconvenient and wasteful of man-power, highlighting the need for a new Headquarters building, and the need for new premises at Ross was also a pressing matter and should be dealt with urgently. Mr. Newton's proposals suggested that the strength of the force required to maintain this level of policing for the county would be one hundred and eighty-nine men plus twelve police-women and fifteen civilians, but the final figure agreed by the Home Office fixed the strength at the higher figure of two hundred and five officers, plus twelve police-women and fifteen civilians.

The merger took effect as planned on 1st. April 1947, and meant that forty-six male and four female officers of Hereford City Police, became members of Herefordshire Constabulary. During the remainder of that year twenty six male and seven female recruits were taken on, eighteen of whom were ex-servicemen, and five were War Reserve officers taking the opportunity to become regulars, and, as previously mentioned, the last officer to return from war service resumed his duties. Four long-serving officers retired on pension during the year, Inspector S.G. Whittaker, PC 57 J. Greenway, Sergeant 101 F.G. Davies, and PC 35 J.J. Chance, and unfortunately the service suffered two deaths, in June, Detective Constable 128 C.A. Nayler, with twenty-three years service, and in December, PC 125 S.C. Colyer, with eighteen years service. Administration of the enlarged Constabulary was carried out from the premises acquired for the purpose at 'Brockington', Hafod Road, Hereford. The new arrangement of Divisions meant the formation of new posts and these were filled as follows:- Chief Inspector F. Wheatley to Superintendent at Central, and Inspector A. Lewis became Superintendent at Ross. PC 119 C.H. Hoskins became Sergeant, and Sergeant F.J. Griffin became Inspector on Traffic, and Detective Constables 18 F.G. Stephens, 124 N.W. Davies and PC 55 D.H. Roberts became the Detective Sergeants of Southern, Central and Northern Divisions respectively.

When the rush of applicants brought about by discharged servicemen seeking a new career was over, the rate of recruiting slowed, and at the end of 1948 there were thirty-eight male vacancies, plus one female and one civilian, and the Chief Constable expressed regret that the educational and physical standards of applicants was low, revealing that out of ninety-three applicants only eighteen had been appointed, with two more transferring from another force. His opinion was that prior to the war many of the best recruits were artisans, and now that there was a labour shortage and workers could take advantage of a five-day week, and extra pay for shift work in industry, the police service did not hold the attraction that it previously had, and until more could be done to make the job attractive to the right type, poor standards of applicant would prevail. Housing was blamed as one of the sources of poor recruitment, and although the number of police-owned houses had increased to forty, and plans were in hand for the construction of twelve houses in

Hereford, those under construction at Eardisley and Upton Bishop were not ready for occupation and there was an immediate need for twenty-seven houses in the county, without taking into account the provision of houses to new recruits if the vacancies were filled by married men. New arrangements at Ross saw the Old Rectory in use as the Divisional office, and a house was taken on rent for the Superintendent. A new rural beat was set up when a council house at Eaton Bishop was allocated for the officer previously stationed at Madley, and part of the old beat went over to the Allensmore officer. The Chief Constable moved from De Lacy House to a house on the outskirts of Hereford which was purchased for his use, and Chief Inspector K.C. Weaver moved into De Lacy House.

All new recruits now attended a thirteen-week training course, followed by a two-week refresher course at the end of their probationary period, and PC 10 S.G. Saunders, of Burley Gate, was seconded to No. 4 Police Training Centre as an Instructor. Sergeant 45 G. Christopher, who at that time was the Divisional Clerk at Leominster, attended the first of the six month Junior courses which were held at the National Police College, Ryton-on-Dunsmore.

Detailed crime figures were made available and indictable crime showed an increase of 9% over the previous year, and a staggering 91.5% increase over 1939, but detection rates increased from the previous year, by 5%, to 60.5%. Five hundred and eighty-nine motoring offences had been dealt with and road accidents numbered seven hundred and thirty-two, a decrease of one hundred from 1947. Three vacancies still existed in the CID, but all members of the department had received specialised training, and had the use of four Ford 10 hp cars, in which over forty-four thousand miles had been covered in 1948. Facilities which existed for the duplication of photographs, were proving very valuable in the distribution of information, as was the availability of the Forensic Science laboratories, whose assistance had been sought on twelve occasions during the year.

Traffic and Communications department had the use of five Austin 16 hp motor cars, two of which were fitted with public address systems, and their patrols of the county covered one hundred and twenty-five thousand miles, in that year. In addition the department was responsible for the maintenance of four Ford cars, a van, a truck and a motor-cycle, which engaged one member of the department almost full-time. Communication was aided by the use of the 'Seven Pillars of Wisdom', the popular name for the pillars installed by the City Police, and now taken into use by the County Constabulary. The pillars, placed at strategic points in the city, and the five police boxes which went with them, were equipped with a blue flashing light and a telephone to contact the patrolling officer, and also a separate telephone for the public to summon assistance, if required. Road awareness was another subject covered by the Traffic Department and was being taught to children. Visits to eleven schools were made, where the pupils took part in practical demonstrations, and the inspection of cycles for road-worthiness, lectures and films on the subject, shown at local cinemas and halls, was part of the programme.

PC 118 D.W. Mauvan, at the King Street pillar, in the early 1950's.

The duties of the Special Constabulary were not now so onerous as during the war years, and there were still four hundred and eighty volunteers who were willing to give up their own time to help out at special functions, when required.

Many changes were under way in 1949, and the first post-war house to be built was finished at Eardisley, and ready for PC 43 G.W. Barker to move into. Several men who already owned, or rented their own houses before joining the service, had helped out the housing situation, but this meant that they were unavailable when moves were in the offing, and so others had to undertake more moves than would have been normal, with all the upheaval to family and schooling that this entailed. Two new houses were being planned for Weobley, and fourteen houses were under construction in Hereford, at Moreland Avenue, Whitecross Road, Vicarage Road and Westfields. Other changes were brought about by the Oaksey Report which made known the findings of the committee set up under the leadership of Lord Oaksey to look into all aspects of police service. Hours of duty, pay and allowances and leave were all considered and the findings came into effect on 1st. July 1949.

An incentive to encourage the future recruitment of an acceptable standard of officer of the future was the introduction of the Police Cadets in 1951. The initial response of applicants was described as 'overwhelming' with the number far exceeding the places available. The Cadets were given experience in clerical duties and all other aspects of police work, and it was hoped that, given a good insight into the job, they would be happy to return to it after the completion of their National Service. In the 1950's several recruits, not only former Cadets, were young men who had just completed their National Service, who in several cases remained on the Army Reserve and were required to attend three annual camps, of two weeks duration. One such former National Serviceman was PC 68 H.B. Carter, who had served with the KSLI from 1949 to 1951, part of which time was spent on active service in Korea. He joined the Constabulary in February 1952, and was stationed at Leominster and Kingsthorne before transferring to the Traffic Department. When police volunteers were called for to assist in the Cyprus emergency in 1956 he was allowed to go, but after only one month in the country he was tragically assassinated in a terrorist attack. His funeral took place at Lyonshall, Herefordshire with more than one hundred of his police colleagues present.

PC 6 C.D. Cook, of Longtown, was seconded to No. 8 District Police Training School as an Instructor in 1952, remaining there until 1955. In 1957 he and his family emigrated to Canada. Formal in-house training, at Headquarters, was a new innovation which was planned to supplement the intermediate and final training of probationers. The officer promoted to Sergeant to undertake this, in 1951, was Detective Constable 131 T.S. Davies, who also took on responsibility for senior constable's refresher courses, and lectures and courses for Police Cadets and Special Constables.

An award to police officers in recognition of long and meritorious service was instituted in 1953, under a warrant made by the late King, George the Sixth, and the first recipients to receive their medals from the Mayor of Hereford, Mr. A.E. Farr, were CC Freeman Newton, KPM, DCC T.B. Wheeler, Det. Insp. R.J. Weaver, Insp. H.J. Harris, BEM, Insp. F.J. Griffin, Insp. G. Christopher, Sgt. B.T. James, Sgt. C.H. Hoskins, Sgt. A. V. Lucas, PC R. Bowler, PC P.T. Jenkins, PC A. Glazzard, PC V.K. Pearce and PC A.

Deakin, former Supt. F. Wheatley, former Sgt. E.J. Cousins, former PC W.H.M. Gould. Similar award ceremonies took place throughout the county; at Leominster-Supt. J.E. Keyte, Insp. F.J. Little, PC W.J. Lines, PC A.E. Matthews and former PC M.A. Barter, at Ledbury-Insp. E.C. Wills, Sgt. F.A. Jackson, former PC C.R. Moody, PC A.F. Rock, PC D. Evans, PC H.J. James, at Harewood End-Sgt. A. Moss, at Ross-Supt. A. Lewis,MM, Insp. D. Grigg and Sgt. H.E.J. Penry, were all presented with their medal.

The coronation of Queen Elizabeth the Second was celebrated in 1953, with the main gatherings in London, necessitating contingents of officers from each police force going to the capital to give assistance with crowd control. A contingent of twenty-two went from Herefordshire, *(names and photograph later in book),* and in addition Coronation medals were presented to eleven regular officers, and five Divisional Commandants, three Inspectors and two Sergeants of the Special Constabulary.

In spite of the very favourable response by the younger generation to enrol as Cadets, the dearth of suitable applicants to become Constables persisted for several years, in fact in one year only seven out of seventy-four applicants were accepted. At the end of 1952 there were eighteen vacancies in the force, twelve of them in the Traffic Department, which was due to undergo large scale change and expansion when the wireless scheme was introduced. The original idea of radio communication in police motor-vehicles had been considered before 1939, but for various reasons was not effected until October 1955, when, as part of a combined scheme, the Police, Fire and Ambulance services and the Electricity Board shared a one hundred and twenty foot mast transmitter, situated seven hundred and forty feet above sea level at Dinmore Hill, and as a result the information room at Headquarters was in twenty-four hour radio contact with the eight vehicles on patrol duty throughout the county. The control room was manned at all times by a Sergeant and a Constable, who were able to trace the movements of vehicles, and direct assistance to wherever it was needed. A plan was also in existence, by which all major services could be co-ordinated from the same control point, in the event of a major incident occurring.

Mr. Freeman Newton was nearing retirement age in 1956, and approached the Standing Joint Committee with a request that his period of service be extended so that he could complete his full thirty years of police service, and also remain in post for the Centenary of the Herefordshire Constabulary which would be celebrated in April 1957. Approval was readily granted for him to remain for one year, at the end of which time the request would be reviewed, in accordance with normal practice.

The Centenary of the Herefordshire Constabulary, the 1st. April 1957, was officially celebrated on Sunday, 7th. April 1957, by a service at Hereford Cathedral, which was attended by all available officers. This was followed by a parade through the city, with a March-Past in High Town, where the salute was taken by Sir Richard Cotterell, Bart., Lord Lieutenant of Herefordshire. At the end of the parade all those taking part formed up for a group photograph. As a further celebration, a booklet prepared by the Chief Constable and Inspector D. Grigg, relating a history of the Constabulary, was distributed to every serving officer.

During what was to be Mr. Newton's final full year of office the establishment of the force was again increased, to two hundred and twenty-eight male officers, twelve female officers, five cadets, and fifteen female civilian staff, out of which there were nineteen vacancies. Although there had been ninety-six applications during that year, only sixteen appointments had been made, fourteen males and two females. The building programme had been completed over the last few years by the completion of the new police stations at Ledbury and Ross, the houses in Hereford and Leominster, Weobley, Ledbury, and Ross and out-stations at Weston-under-Penyard, Whitchurch, Tarrington, Leintwardine, Kingsland, Little Birch, Mansel Lacy and Bishops Frome, and although the Police Authority now owned ninety-eight houses, there was still an urgent estimated need for thirty-nine more.

A new Sub-Division was set up, known as South Wye, to cater for the needs of the growing population of the southern area of the City of Hereford, covered by the two beats of Hinton and Hunderton. Six houses and a new section station were planned, with a Chief Inspector, two Sergeants, eight constables and two police-women providing cover throughout the twenty-four hours. There were thirteen officers now in CID work, and more use was being made of the facilities offered by the Forensic Science Laboratories, and the Midland Regional Clearing House, which had become fully operational in 1956. More than twelve hundred indictable crimes were dealt with in 1957, with a detection rate of sixty per cent. The Traffic Department, with thirty-two officers, and eight cars, covered more than a quarter of a million miles in the course of the year, and fifty-seven arrests were made. More than nine hundred emergency (999) calls had been received and dealt with by the Communications Room.

Mr. Newton was now preparing for his retirement, and a series of resignations and promotions took place. The Deputy Chief Constable, Superintendent T.B. Wheeler, QPM, retired after more than thirty-nine years service, as did Superintendent A. Lewis, MM, at Ross, also with thirty nine years service. Superintendent K.C. Weaver was appointed Deputy Chief Constable, the same position that his father had held, and Inspector C.W. Wallin became Superintendent at Ross, and in all nineteen promotions took place. Two retirements took place at the same time when Sergeant A.V. Lucas retired with thirty years service, and PC 26 C.J. Andrews retired from Burley Gate, after twenty-seven years service.

The Chief Constable had been in Herefordshire for just over thirty years and had overseen, with firmness and dignity, the growth of the Constabulary, the disruption of the war years, the merger with the City Police, and the changes brought about by progress in transport and communications. At a gathering to mark his retirement it was said of him that during his long service he had shown great sympathy towards, and understanding of, his men, and had made the police service in the county 'fit to live and work in'. Further tribute was paid to his contribution to the sporting life of the Constabulary and his concern for welfare. Mrs. Newton also received thanks for the support she had given. In reply Mr. Newton thanked the regular officers, the Special Constabulary and the civilian staff for 'all their loyalty and co-operation'.

HEREFORDSHIRE CONSTABULARY 1958-1967

Robert McCartney, Chief Constable of Herefordshire, 1958-1967.

Robert McCartney was born in Lancashire in 1912, and after a Grammar School education in Blackburn, joined the Lancashire Constabulary in 1930, as a Cadet, becoming a Constable in 1932. He became a Detective Constable and earned his first promotion, to Detective Sergeant, in 1941. In 1947 he gained further promotion, to Inspector, and transferred to the Traffic Department later that year. In 1948 he was promoted to Chief Inspector, later moving to the Special Crime Investigation Squad as Detective Chief Inspector, and second-in-command of Lancashire Criminal Investigation Department. As an expert in criminal law he was, at various times, visiting lecturer at the Lancashire and Liverpool City Police Training Schools. 1955 saw him in command of the Bolton Division as Superintendent, before his move to Monmouthshire in 1956. For five months of his two year tenure of office as Deputy Chief Constable of Monmouthshire, he acted as Chief Constable.
Mr. McCartney was awarded the Queen's Police Medal in January 1962, and in November of the same year he became a Brother of the Order of St. John. He was honoured with the OBE in the New Year Honours List of 1968, immediately after his retirement from the police service in December 1967, and later that year took up his new post as Deputy Governor of the Tower of London. Mr. McCartney died, in Hampshire, at the end of July 1999.

The appointment of Robert McCartney, who was chosen from a 'short-list' of seven, meant that, for the first time, Herefordshire had a Chief Constable who had risen through the ranks, and had experienced at first-hand many aspects of the police service. The Lancashire Constabulary in which he had served for twenty-six years before his brief stay in Monmouthshire, was well known as being in the fore-front of innovation and modernisation. Therefore, bearing in mind the contrast of the large and forward-thinking Constabulary from which he came, compared to the size of the one he took over, some of the ideas which Mr. McCartney proposed for rural Herefordshire were seen, at the time, as revolutionary, and out of keeping for the area. The formation of the West Mercia Constabulary was then unforeseen, but with hindsight it can be said that the changes Mr. McCartney introduced helped to propel Herefordshire Constabulary into the modern age and ensured that when the merger took place nine years later, the members of the Herefordshire Constabulary were as far ahead with new methods of policing as were their counterparts in other counties.

One of the matters causing concern to Mr. McCartney was the great increase in road traffic, meaning that all officers were spending more time on traffic related matters, including controlling parking and pedestrian crossings, and most importantly attending to road accidents which were increasing, to a total of one thousand three hundred and sixty-five in 1958, compared with just over seven hundred ten years earlier. The Chief Constable expressed a hope that the motoring public would respond by careful driving and observance of the regulations, and hoped that police time could be spent in other ways which would be of more benefit to the public.

At the end of 1958, when Mr. McCartney had been in post for six months, he reported that from a total authorised strength of two hundred and forty there were vacancies for twenty-two regular officers and two civilian staff. During the year there had been ninety-nine applicants, from whom nine had been appointed, with two others transferring from other constabularies. Seven officers retired on pension, eight resigned for various reasons and Sergeant 56 L.A. Workman, the Divisional Clerk at Leominster, who had begun his police career as Junior Clerk in July 1934, sadly passed away in April. In July 1958 PC 67 S. Roberts was seconded to the British Police Unit in Cyprus for a period of twenty-one months, in response to a request for three hundred officers from this country.

The high number of vacancies in the Constabulary continued throughout the following year, reaching the highest point that it had been since the end of the war. One of the reasons given for low recruitment, apart from the unsuitability of many candidates, was the fact that industry was offering higher wages and in many areas there was full employment, therefore there were few workers seeking an alternative. The inability of the Police Authority to provide adequate, modern housing was another deterrent to recruitment, although the situation was helped in 1959 by the completion of ten new houses in Hereford, four at Bromyard, and new out-stations at Bredenbury and Wellington, with more planned for Hereford (South Wye), Ross-on-Wye, Bodenham, Clifford, Ewyas Harold, St. Weonards and Kington. Many of the older properties in the county were still in use, and in some localities, even where the house itself was good, the facilities in the rural areas were sadly lacking. Electricity was gradually being laid on to most of rural Herefordshire, but in some of the more remote areas was still several years away. Water supply was the biggest problem for police families, and the occupants of at least one station collected water from a communal tap, with several others such as Kingsthorne, Upton Bishop and Burley Gate relying on an outdoor pump, or the comparative luxury of an indoor pump in the kitchen, and in dry weather supplies brought by bowser to fill the well. This situation continued, at some village stations, until the middle of the nineteen-sixties.

A scheme, submitted by the Chief Constable, and approved by the Standing Joint Committee outlined a re-organisation, whereby the Wigmore Section merged with Leominster Section, and the Bredwardine and Abbeydore Sections were combined. Some out-station beats merged, others were redesigned and the officers were made more mobile by the introduction of six radio-equipped motor-cycles. The overall plan meant a reduction in the total strength by five Constables. The arrangement was greeted with consternation by some rural communities who regarded their resident policeman as an essential part of the village scene, but were reassured by Mr. McCartney's reply to their complaint, in which he pointed out that times and places had changed greatly since the original beat system was set up, and now that there was a county-wide radio link available, he felt that it should be utilised to a greater extent. Another point he made was that because the off-duty time of police-officers had increased, some beats could be left without cover for several days, whereas with a mobile beat officer available an immediate response could be given. The first six officers to attend a motor-cycle training course at the Glamorgan Constabulary Motor School were PCs 180 M.R. Wood, (Pembridge), 44 G.R. Gough, (Upton Bishop), 184 F.G. Daniels, (Orleton), 49 J. Down, (Harewood End), 113 G.J. Wood, (Bringsty), and 34 G. Sanders, (Peterchurch), who were ready to take to the road in October 1960, on their 'Velocette' motor-cycles, sometimes known as 'Whispering Ghosts', because of their very low noise level.

The new mobile system, and the opening of South Wye Police Station early in 1960, together with extra motor patrol work caused by the opening of the twenty-one mile Ross Spur Motorway in November, which was shared with the police of the neighbouring counties of Worcestershire and Gloucestershire, had called for re-organisation of man-power, and again high-lighted the shortages. It was hoped that the findings of a Royal Commission which was set up in 1960 to look at aspects of the police service, nationally, including pay and conditions, the functioning of Police Authorities, and the relationship between the police and public, would improve conditions of service and act as a spur to recruiting. Later that year pay increases were announced resulting in a marked increase in applications to join the Constabulary in 1961, when there were one hundred and forty applicants, of whom twenty were appointed.

The Deputy Chief Constable, Superintendent K.C. Weaver retired in June 1960, and Superintendent C.W. Wallin was appointed Deputy in his place. Chief Inspector D.A. Pickard was promoted to Superintendent and took over command of Southern Division at Ross. Detective Constable 67 S. Roberts returned to Hereford from his secondment to Cyprus, and Detective Sergeant 141 K. Lawley, who had been in charge of Central Division CID, flew off to Nyasaland as part of the British Police mission. Sergeant 131 T. S., Davies was seconded to No. 8 District Training School, as an Instructor, where he remained until his retirement in 1963. Approval was given for the appointment of three officers to the First Police Reserve, which was open to police officers who had retired, and were still physically fit. Former Sergeant 119 C.H. Hoskins took up duties at the Police garage as FRPC 1, and a former police officer from Birmingham City, H.G. Bull, became FRPC 2 at South Wye Police Station. FRPC Bull died in February 1963, and was replaced by former PC 126 R.J. Garrett.

In March 1961, the Dean of Hereford, the Very Reverend Hedley R. Burrows, who was in his final year as Dean of Hereford, visited Police Headquarters to dedicate a joint memorial to all members of the Herefordshire Constabulary and Hereford City Police, who had given their lives in two World Wars, and at the same time a separate memorial was dedicated to Hugh Brian Carter who lost his life whilst serving with the British Police Mission to Cyprus.

Noticeably on the increase was the disregard of motoring regulations, which was being dealt with by prosecutions and letters of caution to motorists. A spate of minor crime, prevalent throughout the country, was recognised as being a particular nuisance in the central part of Herefordshire, with the increasing totals of house and shop-breaking offences causing the most alarm. The Chief Constable considered that Crime Prevention was of great importance and Detective Sergeant 152 J.F.G. Barnett attended a Crime Prevention Study Course in Shropshire. Other officers undertook training courses at a variety of other training establishments, including the Police College, the Birmingham City Police School, the Civil Defence Staff College and the Civil Defence Training School at Falfield. A purpose-built Training Wing was in use at Headquarters, and had been opened in August 1959 by W.H. Cornish, CB, an Under Secretary of State. The courses organised there included weekly Directed Study for Promotion courses, further training for Probationary Constables and Directed Study for Cadets, and in addition courses for Special Constables had been arranged during the Winter. Under a local review of the Special Constabulary a number had been invited to resign, when it was found that some were over the age limit of sixty-five years, or were unable to perform duties because of personal circumstances, but a recruiting drive brought in adequate numbers to take their places, and the number available for duty stood at around three hundred, out of a possible establishment of six hundred and fifty.

Civil Defence Training was now very much to the fore, because of the Cold War, and the threats involved, and all senior officers were required to attend a training course at the Civil Defence Staff College. Former Inspector H.J. Harris, who had been seconded from police duties in 1953, for the final year of his twenty-five years service, in order to take up the new post of County Civil Defence Officer, continued to be responsible for Civil Defence arrangements throughout the county. Six officers attended Warden Section Instructor Courses at the Falfield School, in Gloucestershire, while others were trained locally. A Regional Police Mobile Column had been set up, for the purpose of assisting at any emergency, and two Sergeants and eight Constables attached to the Mobile Column attended a refresher course at Headquarters Training School in 1963. The siren warning system, disused since the end of the war, was updated and responsibility for its maintenance passed to the Police Authority. The system was later expanded to key out-stations where a mobile siren was kept, for use in emergency, and almost one hundred carrier line broadcast receivers were installed, many of them at out-stations throughout the county, which were ideally situated to spread a warning, should the need arise. Six-monthly tests of these receivers were carried out, involving a broadcast message which had to be judged for clarity. The training of instructors was extended, and two groups of officers qualified as Civil Defence Warden Section Instructors, after training which took place partly at Civil Defence Headquarters in Hereford, and partly at Police Headquarters, under the Training Officer (Civil Defence) of the time, Sergeant 57 P.J. Noakes. The newly trained officers were, in turn, responsible for recruiting and training wardens and

Special Constables, on their own beats. The nine who qualified in January 1965 were PCs 159 J.C.C. Cole, (Tarrington), 70 P.J. Knight, (Hereford City) 173 E.A. Hadley, (Burley Gate), 187 H.I. Evans, (Leintwardine), 181 B.K. Herbert, (Eardisley), 96 A.C. Smith, (Clifford), 192 R.M. Parker, (Pontrilas), 36 G.T. Lewis, (Kingsthorne) and 193 D.G. Craig, (Cradley).

The Royal Commission, which had been set up in 1960, made its report in 1963, a year in which much vilification of the police service nationally took place, much of it unfounded, but some, unfortunately, was found to have substance. The findings of the Commission, which were mainly complimentary to the police and were not as a result of any adverse publicity appertaining to the service, advocated many administrative changes thought to be worthy of consideration, and high-lighted the difficulties encountered by the police in the recent past, which were outlined in the Police Bill presented to Parliament. One particular recommendation, which was to prove very significant in this county, was that some of the smaller Constabularies should be amalgamated. The Police Act became law on 10th. June 1964, and its content clarified and consolidated practices and arrangements which had come into use over the long life of the police service, many of which had been recommended to the Commission by the various Authorities. The Act further stipulated that from 1st. June 1965 Standing Joint Committees would be replaced by Police Committees of the County Councils, made up of two-thirds County Council members, and one-third from the Magistrates.

It became compulsory for every Chief Constable to submit an Annual Report, which hitherto had not been done in every Constabulary. The practice had been in existence in Herefordshire from the early 1900s, and Mr. McCartney's report for 1964 gave his usual very full description of the work of the Constabulary during the year. A forty-two hour working week had been introduced in July 1964, and the establishment of the Constabulary was increased during the year by five Sergeants and thirty-four Constables, making the authorised strength two hundred and fifty-seven males, twelve female officers, three First Police Reserve officers, twenty clerks and typists, twelve Police Cadets, and one groundsman/caretaker. Actual numbers fell short of this by fifty male and three female Constables, and one Cadet. Although the building programme continued, about twenty officers were still in accommodation not owned by the Police Authority, but fifteen officers were helping the situation by living in their own houses. The house at Clifford had been completed, and a new Police Station and house at Peterchurch was under way, with another house planned for Brimfield. The site anticipated for the Divisional Headquarters at Leominster had been found to be unsuitable, but the availability of an alternative site was being negotiated, and the possibility of a Traffic Headquarters at Newtown Road, Hereford was being discussed.

Traffic offences during the year showed an appreciable increase over the five year average, with the biggest increase in cases of dangerous or careless driving. The use of a Radar Speed Meter proved to be effective in detecting speeding road-users, and meant that there could be a reduction in man-power employed on that task, than would previously have been necessary in order to obtain the same results. The meter had been hired for six months, and arrangements were made to obtain its use for a full year.

Towards the end of 1964 the Chief Constable was partially seconded to the Police

College, for about nine months, to take over as Director of the Senior Staff Course, and arrangements were made that during his absence the daily duties of running the Constabulary were taken over by the Deputy Chief Constable, C.W. Wallin. Superintendent T. Rees took over temporary duties at Headquarters, and Chief Inspector R.G. Kendle, became acting Superintendent, at Central Division.

With more emphasis being placed on training than ever before, the numbers who were being trained locally made it necessary to consider extending the training wing at Headquarters. The approved establishment of Cadets was increased during 1965 from twelve to eighteen, and their training courses continued at Headquarters, as well as external studies at the College of Further Education, where many of them obtained GCE passes. In addition to their introduction to police work the Cadets had drill and exercises, physical training, First Aid instruction, and swimming, as part of their normal curriculum and were encouraged to participate in The Duke of Edinburgh award scheme. In 1965 a total of eighty-six officers, including thirty-two new recruits on Initial Training Courses at Bridgend, Glamorgan, attended courses at external training establishments for varying lengths of time, on subjects as varied as CID, Scene of Crime, advanced driving, and motor-cycle training. Crime Prevention training was undertaken to extend the department which had been set up in 1964, with PC 100 N.G. Ovens as the first Crime Prevention Officer. Nearly two hundred personnel received instruction at the training wing on short courses, as well as about the same number of Special Constables who had their usual winter training sessions. Civil Defence Training was continued by one hundred and seventy-nine regular officers who attended local two-day refresher courses.

The absence from normal duties of so many personnel put a strain on available man-power, which still showed a deficiency, of thirty, and to help alleviate the situation the 'Robophone' system of answering and recording telephone calls was installed at Ledbury, Kington and Bromyard Section Stations, in an effort to make more officers available for patrol duty. The experiment was judged to be a success, and was expected to be more acceptable when the officers at those stations also had the use of personal radio. A brief trial of personal radio had already taken place with sets which were on loan, and an initial supply, purchased for use at Hereford, Leominster and Ross-on-Wye, proved successful after some early problems.

PC 117 A.G.W. Matthews, trying out a personal radio.

A popular scheme was introduced which allowed officers nearing retirement to move out of police property and purchase their own house, which was seen as a possible way to ease the pressure on police housing. The following year the number of years service required to qualify for this privilege was set at fifteen. More police officers were now adequately housed than ever before, although thirteen officers were still classed as being in sub-standard accommodation, and advantage was taken of Local Authority house building schemes at Ledbury and Ross-on-Wye, whereby houses were allocated for police use.

A Police Advisory Board, set up in 1965, studied man-power problems, organisation, and the need to modernise the equipment available to the police service. In a considered reply to the report, Mr. McCartney expressed his opinion to the Police

Committee that he thought that the police service could not continue to carry out the myriad tasks which were thrust upon it, in some cases because the responsibility did not fit into the remit of any other branch of public service. In many cases the laws they were trying to enforce were many years out of date, and remained unchanged in a society which was changing rapidly.

Further addressing the Police Committee, the Chief Constable spoke with regret of the announcement made on 18th. May 1966, that Herefordshire Constabulary was being forced 'voluntarily' to arrange an amalgamation with the Shropshire and Worcestershire Constabularies, and Worcester City Police. He pointed out that the Home Secretary did not imply inefficiency of smaller Constabularies, but was of the opinion that the combining of a larger area to be policed by a single unit, would be conducive to efficiency. Mr. McCartney went on to refer to the time, one hundred and ten years previously, when the population of Herefordshire received the formation of the Constabulary with antagonism, but felt that the intervening time had changed opinions, so that most of the population were satisfied with, and supported, the Constabulary which had evolved. He regretted that Herefordshire Constabulary would cease to exist on the 1st. October 1967.

Despite the fact that Herefordshire Constabulary was to cease to function within a fairly short time, and, behind the scenes, plans for the merger were going ahead, progress continued and the introduction of new methods of policing gathered pace. Traffic Wardens, a uniformed service, suitably trained, but without police qualifications, had been operating since the early 1960's in towns and cities elsewhere in the country, but only to the extent that they dealt with stationary traffic, parking offences and obstruction, and it had been felt that the need did not exist in Herefordshire. However, where employed, they had proved to be very successful, and their duties had released uniformed officers for their true function of prevention and detection of crime. In June 1965 the range of duties of Wardens was increased, to include the control of moving traffic, and the fixed penalty scheme was introduced. Soon after this, on the Secretary of State's recommendation, a Working Party was formed to consider their use in Herefordshire, and the findings, published in December 1965, recommended that fourteen Wardens should be employed as soon as possible, ten in Hereford, two in Ross, and two in Leominster. With the approval of the Secretary of State, and an extension of the fixed penalty system the scheme was ready to go ahead. A former police house, No. 11 De Lacy Street, one of the original City Police/Firemen's houses built in 1885, was no longer required for housing purposes, and was taken over as office accommodation for the Traffic Wardens. PC 45 W. M. Cain had been promoted to Sergeant at the end of 1966, with responsibility for the Traffic Wardens, and a Clerk/Typist was appointed in May 1967, twelve days prior to the appointment of the first ten Traffic Wardens. Eight were designated to work in Hereford and two in Ross-on-Wye, and, after two weeks training at Headquarters, their formal duties began on 1st. June 1967. Initially they dealt only with breaches of parking regulations and gave advice to offenders, but after two weeks the fixed penalty system was implemented. In Hereford, point-duty and the control of the traffic flow, carried out by the Wardens, was of great importance, to enable the new traffic arrangements devised by the City Council to be brought into use, allowing the contractors to begin work on the new relief road, planned to follow the line of the mediaeval city walls.

The advent of the Traffic Wardens in Hereford and Ross, while not pleasing all of the motoring public, had the immediate effect of helping to ease the flow of traffic and of freeing parking places, particularly in Hereford city centre, so that more vehicles were able to be parked for a short time. Inevitably there were complaints, but after a short time, when the motorists began to feel the benefit of the changes, and realised that Traffic Wardens were here to stay, they adapted to the new system.

One of the original number, P.N. Davies, resigned and was replaced before the merger in September, and the ten who transferred to West Mercia Constabulary were:

TW 1 D.T. Barrington
TW 2 G.D. Begg
TW 3 W.M. Mason
TW 4 P.S. Everson
TW 5 R.F. Griffin
TW 6 M.J. Hart
TW 7 A.R. Humphries
TW 8 A.D. Aston
TW 9 J.J. Bishop
TW 10 E.M. Sheldrick

The time which the police in Hereford had formerly spent on traffic control, was utilised to good effect by the introduction of the Neighbourhood Beat system, which after some delay, awaiting the delivery of the necessary personal radios, finally began on 14th. August 1967. Six beats on the outskirts of the city, each with a resident Constable, were formed into three units, two of them north of the river, and the third on the south of the City. Discretionary working was introduced and each Constable covered his beat on foot or cycle, with additional twenty-four hour cover by a unit car. The cars which were used for patrol, each with a team of five drivers, were easily recognised by their distinctive blue and white pattern, and quickly earned the name 'Panda' cars. The personal radio enabled every officer on duty to be in constant touch with his control point, and to make use of a talk-through facility with his colleagues on the beat, resulting in a quicker response time to any incident requiring police attendance. In an interview at the time, Mr. McCartney stressed the importance of a constable being familiar with his own 'patch', and said that the aim of the neighbourhood beat system was to step up the police service in the city and 'to try and develop a friendship between the policeman and the public'. The Chief Constable went on to emphasise what an officer in a Panda car could do to cut down vandalism and petty theft in Hereford, and he hoped that the police and public could combine to make 'immediate and substantial attacks on wasteful and senseless anti-social epidemics wherever they break out'.

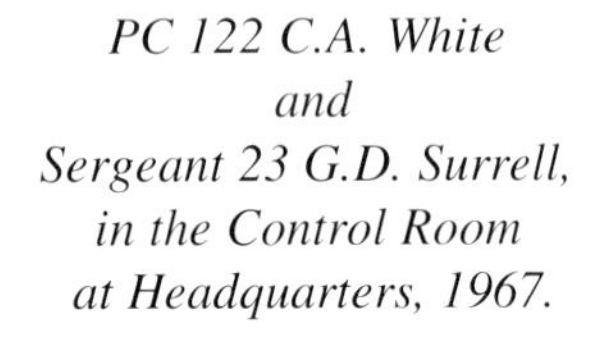

*PC 122 C.A. White
and
Sergeant 23 G.D. Surrell,
in the Control Room
at Headquarters, 1967.*

In July 1967 three Constables began a three month Dog Handlers course at Worcester, where, after building up a mutual friendship and trust between man and animal, they were trained together in all aspects of tracking, searching and patrol work. The three officers, with their German Shepherd dogs were: PC 36 G.T. Lewis and Simba, PC 42 D. T. Allen and Major and PC 186 J.E.G. Prescott and Buck. They did not perform any duty together until after the merger.

Promotions and moves were necessary so that all officers were ready to start with the new organisation on 1st. October. The Chief Constable of the new West Mercia Constabulary, Mr. John A. Willison, was appointed, and the whole of the county of Herefordshire was designated 'E' Division, with the exception of the Ledbury area in the east of the county, and the two northern beats of Wigmore and Leintwardine. The principal officers were named as:

Chief Superintendent C.W. Wallin, in charge of 'E' Division. *(Herefordshire)*
Superintendent T. Rees, Deputy in charge 'E' Division. *(Herefordshire)*
Detective Chief Inspector C. Lappage, in charge CID. *(Herefordshire)*
Chief Inspector F.A. Boughton, in charge Traffic Department
Chief Inspector J. Keyte, in charge Hereford Sub-Division, *(Herefordshire)*
Chief Inspector R.N. Blythe, in charge Leominster Sub-Division
Chief Inspector G.P. Morris, in charge Ross Sub Division. *(Herefordshire)*

Herefordshire Constabulary was about to pass into history, and the county of Hereford would become one of many Divisions, as part of one of the biggest territorial Police Districts in the country. Understandably, there was a feeling of sorrow, and apprehension about the future. More than eleven hundred and thirty men and forty-one women had served as regular officers, from the first one appointed by Captain Telfer early in 1857, to the last one appointed by Chief Constable McCartney in September, 1967. One officer served for sixty years, and another served for one day, and was allowed to resign, providing he refunded the two shillings and six-pence paid to the Police Surgeon, but they, and all the others helped to make up the history of the Constabulary. More than thirty years have passed since then, and the first recruits to join West Mercia Constabulary are probably themselves pensioners. Everyone has his own feelings as to whether the inevitable step was for the better, but all can look back with pride on their connection, close or distant, with the Herefordshire Constabulary.

CIVILIAN STAFF.

Prior to 1928 when the first Junior Clerk was employed there had been no civilian help employed by the Herefordshire Constabulary since its formation seventy years previously. Any manual jobs needed, chopping firewood, whitewashing cells, polishing desks and doorknobs was done by whoever happened to be on duty, a situation which continued into the 1950's at smaller Section Stations. These jobs eventually became the responsibility of many part-time domestic workers and other ancillary staff, who quickly proved to be indispensable. The main change with clerical staff had come after the Second War when it had been realised how useful and reliable civilians had been, and from the six clerical staff employed in 1946, the figure doubled by the next year. The numbers increased as new departments were set up, and clerks and typists played their part in the ever increasing work of the police service. Eventually civilians began to take over some jobs which had previously only been done only by regular officers, thereby releasing them for normal police duties.

Civilians who transferred to West Mercia Constabulary, on 30th. September 1967 :

K.M. McKenzie
B.E. Parry
K.J. Robbins
A.F. Vose-Davies
G.M. Harding
N.H. Bassett
L. Hoskins
B. Lowe
J.J. McKenna
I.J. Orpe
D.M. Woodman
K.M. Davies
J.H. Thomas
G.E. Williams
C.A. Jackson
R. Gough
A. Stewart
C.A. Woodman
W.J. Ridler
L. Dodgson
A. Holt
M.J. Lewis
M. Baker

POLICE CADETS.

Fourteen Police Cadets transferred to West Mercia Constabulary at the end of September 1967. The education and activities of Cadets has been described earlier, and proved to be a valuable foundation for those former Cadets who chose to make the police service their career, or went into other walks of life.

R.A. Hanks
J.B. Scandrett
R.C. Norman
J.M. Davies
L.J. Davies
B.C. Hill
P.J. Warren
T.A. McAvoy
J.B. Maddrell
J.R. Green
G.G. Mansfield
E. Clements
H.D. Jones
R.F. Bray

Nominal Roll of Officers serving in the Herefordshire Constabulary on 30th. September 1967

Chief Constable: R. McCartney, QPM.
Superintendent and Deputy Chief Constable: C.W. Wallin.
Superintendents: T. Rees, L.H. Jones, J.E. Orme.

Chief Inspectors: J. Keyte, G. Painter, C.H. Lappage, J.H. Westwood.

Inspectors: E. Cobbe, S. Whittall, G.P. Morris, J.F. Barnett, A.W.C. Morris, J.R. Clinton, S.G. Perks, B. Gradwell, N.G. Ovens.

Sergeants and Constables

P.S. 2 L.T. Whitworth
P.C. 3 R. Taylor
P.C. 4 J. Dowson
P.C. 5 D.W. Jones
P.C. 6 T.J. Curtis
P.C. 7 M.J. Hopkins
P.S. 8 A.J. Williams
P.C. 9 B.G. Mayne
P.S. 10 B.S. Williams
P.C. 11 R.N. Lane
P.C. 12 D.G. Pascoe
P.C. 13 W.A. Barker
D.C. 14 R. Duggan
D.C. 15 W.J. Booth
P.C. 16 P.R. Parry
P.C. 17 J.P.C. Dolan
P.C. 18 K.J. Hursey
P.S. 19 H.J. Cole
P.C. 20 R.I. Matthews
P.S. 21 J.S. Bourne
P.C. 22 J.A. Bull
P.S. 23 G.D. Surrell
P.S. 24 H.L. Watkins
P.C. 25 T.R. Mash
P.C. 26 J.F. Dawes
D.S. 27 B.A. Smith
P.C. 28 R.I. Scott
P.S. 29 B.D. Stephenson
P.C. 30 J.D. Owen
P.C. 31 D.S.G. Hughes
P.C. 32 E.H.J. Clinton
P.S. 33 M.W. Kidd
P.C. 34 G. Sanders
P.C. 36 G.T. Lewis
P.C. 37 N.J.B. Outram
P.C. 38 P. Feakes
P.S. 39 R.J. Farmer
P.C. 40 D.J. Jordan
P.C. 41 G.T. Cousins
P.C. 42 D.T. Allen
P.C. 43 W.T. Walker
P.S. 44 G.R. Gough
P.C. 45 W.M. Cain
P.C. 46 R.G. Brown
P.C. 47 R. Morris
P.S. 48 M.T. Ovens
P.C. 49 J.H. Down
P.S. 50 G. Lawrence
P.C. 51 C.C. Boughton
P.C. 52 C.H.W. Maddy
P.C. 53 R.D. Boulter
P.C. 54 G.A. Archer
P.S. 55 G.M. Brace
P.C. 56 R.C. Wood
P.S. 57 P.J. Noakes
P.C. 58 C. Wells
P.C. 59 J.R.E. Berwick
P.C. 60 R.E. Baylis
P.C. 61 K. Baker
D.C. 62 R.J. Probert
P.C. 63 R.C. Short
P.S. 64 L.T. Bowdley
P.C. 65 A.J. Haynes
P.C. 66 J.L.N. Osborn
P.S. 67 S. Roberts
P.C. 68 E.J. Price
P.S. 69 D.G. Jones
P.C. 70 P.J. Knight
P.C. 71 T.W. Button
P.C. 72 J.S.M. Morris
P.S. 73 J.W.G. Densham
D.C. 74 M. Gibbons
P.C. 75 W.T. Turbutt
P.C. 76 G.T. Warley
P.C. 77 R.J.T. Jones
P.C. 78 J.C. Vernalls
P.C. 79 C.W. Marsh
P.C. 80 P.J. Burley
P.C. 81 E. Owen
P.C. 82 P. Phillips
P.C. 83 D.C. Parker
P.C. 84 W.D. Deakin
P.C. 85 A.H. Cousins
P.C. 86 P.J. Wilkinson
P.C. 87 W.J. Williams
P.C. 88 B. Gutteridge
P.C. 89 K.F. Brooks
P.C. 90 S.G. Brace
P.S. 91 K.W. Campbell
P.C. 92 J. Cook
D.C. 93 D.J. Powell
P.C. 94 W.J. Mercer
P.C. 95 C. Holmes
P.C. 96 A.C. Smith
P.S. 97 G.A. Birch
P.C. 98 C.H.J. Day
P.C. 99 G.F. Middleton
D.S. 101 J.O. Young
P.C. 102 C.F. Stubbs
D.S. 103 P. Devenish
P.C. 104 R.J. Kedward
P.C. 105 D.H. Thomas
P.C. 106 C.G. Davies
P.C. 107 T.R. Tipton
D.C. 108 C. Furber
P.S. 109 M.J. Read
P.C. 110 M.W. Wood
P.C. 111 E. McMenamin
P.C. 112 A.E. Barnes
P.C. 113 M.A. Woodhall
P.C. 114 T. Allen
P.C. 115 D.C. Tibbles
P.C. 116 A.J. Mumford
P.C. 117 A.G.W. Matthews
P.C. 118 D.W. Mauvan
P.C. 119 M.J. Moxham
P.C. 120 S.E. Baggett

P.C. 121 A.P. Mason
P.C. 122 C.A. White
P.C. 123 V. Davies
P.C. 124 D. Price
P.C. 125 D.C.S. Carter
P.C. 126 T.A.J. Williams
P.C. 127 G.R. Thwaites
P.C. 128 F. Neal
P.C. 129 L.H. Taylor
P.C. 130 W.G. Hill
P.C. 131 B.S. Humphreys
P.C. 132 D.R. Tomkins
P.C. 133 M.G. Broad
P.C. 134 C.V. Lloyd
P.S. 135 A. Harding
P.C. 136 A. Howls
P.C. 137 K.R. Pearson
P.S. 138 A.G. Roberts
P.C. 139 D.F. Willett
P.C. 140 D.C. Morgan
P.C. 141 R.A. Parry
D.S. 142 A. Benbow
P.C. 143 E.L. Stainer
P.S. 144 K.W. Norris
P.S. 145 L.F. Morrisey
P.S. 146 D.W. Evans
P.C. 147 W.A. Reid
P.C. 148 J.A. Breeze
P.C. 149 G.N. Murrie
P.C. 150 C.G. Symonds
P.C. 151 J.J. Preece
P.C. 152 G. Lewis
P.C. 153 G.J. Nash
P.S. 154 A.W. Sherred
P.C. 155 W.J. Hillstead
P.C. 156 P.N. Foskett
P.C. 157 J.H. Whent
P.C. 158 D.W. Pikes
P.S. 159 J.C.C. Cole
P.C. 160 F. Davies
P.C. 161 L.A. Sparrow
P.C. 162 C. Joyce
P.C. 163 F. Evans
P.C. 164 D.A.L. Johnson
P.C. 165 P.S. Warrington
P.C. 166 T.C. Walters
P.C. 167 F.R. Powell
P.C. 168 M.J. Cowley
P.C. 169 W. Wallace
P.S. 170 J.P. Bayford
P.C. 171 C.B. Wood
P.C. 172 W.J. Osborn
P.C. 173 E.A. Hadley
P.C. 174 G. Mason
P.C. 175 D.A.M. Mitton
D.S. 176 A.P. Paton
P.C. 177 D.G. Banks
P.C. 178 J.A.M. Main
P.C. 179 J. Kelly
P.C. 180 R.S. Kitching
P.C. 181 B.K. Herbert
D.C. 182 F.J. Joseph
P.C. 183 G.B. Tipton
P.C. 184 F.G. Daniels
P.C. 186 J.E.G. Prescott
P.C. 187 H.I. Evans
P.C. 188 P.A. Holman
P.C. 189 R.J. Williams
P.S. 190 B.W. Thomas
P.C. 191 D.J.T. Talbot
P.C. 192 R.M. Parker
P.C. 193 D.G. Craig
P.C. 194 P.B.P. Holman
P.C. 195 P.G. Hicks
P.C. 196 G. Daniels
P.C. 197 G. Davies
P.C. 198 G.R. Stevenson
P.C. 199 G.I. Evans
P.C. 200 J.B. Jones
P.C. 201 G.S. Millichip
P.C. 202 D.L. Harrison
P.C. 203 R.M. Renouf
P.C. 204 R.J. Wood
P.C. 205 T.J. Thomas
P.C. 206 C.B. Pearce
P.C. 207 J.E. Taylor
P.C. 208 R.P. Rees
P.C. 210 B.J.C. Smith
P.C. 211 M.B. Wood
P.C. 212 D.M. Davies
P.C. 213 G.W. Corfield
P.C. 214 T.S. Moses

Policewomen

P.W. 1 M.T. Powell
P.W. 2 M.A. Lloyd
P.W. 4 M.T. Oxton
P.W.S.5 D. Slater
P.W. 6 N.M. Brace
P.W. 7 O.M. Hughes
P.W. 8 J.L. Lloyd
P.W. 9 M.C. Nelson
P.W. 11 E.S. Phillips
P.W. 12 M.A. Powell

First Police Reserve

R.P.C. 1 C.H. Hoskins
R.P.C. 2 R.J. Garrett

UNIFORMS and INSIGNIA – 1857 to 1967.

When the Constabulary was formed in Herefordshire in 1857 it was fortunate that uniforms had been well tried and tested by other Forces founded earlier, and there would have been a choice as to suitability and cost, to fulfil the needs of a County Constabulary. It should be pointed out that in the early days police officers were obliged to wear uniform at all times, except in bed! These instructions were not withdrawn until late in the 19th Century, when civilian clothes were allowed to be worn on days off.

Early records do not describe the original uniforms issued in Herefordshire, but an inventory of the entitlement of each officer reads as follows:

1 Great Coat	1 Stock	1 Staff
3 Pairs Trousers	1 Whistle	1 Pair Handcuffs
2 Dress Coats	1 Lanthorn	1 Instruction Book
2 Hats	1 Cape	1 Warrant Card

It can be assumed that the uniform was of the type that was in general use at the time – a knee-length wide-skirted tunic, with eight black buttons, fastened to the neck, with the officers numerals and the letters HCC on the collar band. This would be completed by a leather belt with a 'snake' fastener, which was not only decorative, but also supported the 'Bulls-Eye' oil lantern. This type of belt continued to be worn until the early 1920's. It is possible that a top-hat was worn originally, but the 'Shako' type helmet with a Victorian crown badge was being worn by the early 1870's.
Constables and Sergeants continued to wear the same style of tunic until about 1895, with the Sergeant's chevrons being worn on the lower right sleeve.

PC 32 W. Dykes, about 1882

Superintendent John Phillips. Joined Herefordshire Constabulary in 1862, and was transferred to Radnorshire, by Captain Telfer, for just over one year. He returned to Herefordshire, and retired in 1909, after forty-seven years service,

He died in 1910

The Superintendent's uniform consisted of a plain frock coat, with concealed fastening, worn without a belt. Initially the Superintendent wore no badge of rank.

1857. In his first report, in October, HM Inspector of Constabulary stated that the uniforms and equipment were of good quality.

1859. A Boot allowance of six pence per week was granted, but by 1861 the allowance had been reduced to sixteen shillings per annum.

PC 54 J. Broad, with the new style helmet

About 1889. The helmet of the type we know today, fitted with a 'Rose' ventilator and metal band, was issued. The badge also changed to a wreath with a scroll HC in the centre, surmounted by a Victorian crown. (The Hampshire Constabulary wore a similar helmet plate). It has often been queried whether the scroll letters represent the letters HC or HCC, ie Herefordshire Constabulary or Hereford County Constabulary, bearing in mind that the letters HCC were worn on the collar band of the tunic and overcoat of Sergeants and Constables until 1928, when one letter C was dropped. It has been checked with calligraphers and others who agree that the lettering is HC only.

About 1892. Photographs show whistle chains being worn for the first time. Whistles had been issued from the time of the formation of the force, but these must have been concealed and were probably of the 'pea-whistle' type. The 'air-whistles' with chains, which were on issue until recent times, came into use in London about 1884. It was several years later that they came into general use.

Victoria Crown Cap Badge

PC 23 P. Taylor

1896/7. A new, shorter Grenadier Guard type tunic, fastened to the neck, with eight metal buttons was issued. The Sergeant's chevrons were moved from the lower sleeve to just above the elbow. HC was on the helmet plate and HCC on the collar band

PC 12 W. Howard

alongside the officers number.
A lighter weight tunic was also issued, fastened to the neck, with five metal buttons. This tunic was worn without a belt, and presumably was for summer wear. The overcoats then being worn had a Prussian style collar, double-breasted, and buttoned to the neck, with two rows of six buttons. HCC and numerals were on the collar and a belt was worn. The Superintendent's uniform remained unchanged.

1904. A photograph taken then shows sergeants and constables wearing leather gaiters. Presumably, as they were also wearing overcoats, the gaiters were for winter wear. *(The photograph appears later in the book).*

1904/5. The pill-box hat, for summer wear, and tunics with two breast pockets, seven metal buttons and no belt, with each sleeve trimmed with braid, were introduced. *(See group photo below).* In order to qualify for the First Aid badge, which was worn on the right sleeve, officers had taken a St. John's Ambulance Association course, and examination, certificated on passing. Both the cap badge and helmet plate bore the Tudor (King's) crown, instead of the Victorian crown. Just prior to the first World War a shorter style tunic, fastened to the neck with concealed fasteners, two breast pockets, and worn without a belt, was worn by some Superintendents, although until 1925 others continued to wear the frock coat with, sometimes, the crown badge on each shoulder. The badge of rank on the new tunics was a crown on each epaulette.

Bromyard Division, 1913
Back row, L. to R. PCs 45 A.Oakley, 25 J. Edge, 72 S. Wynn, 29 E. Jarrett, 46 J. Prosser, 60 B. Hackett
Front row, L. to R. Sergeant 67 D. Thomas, Superintendent J. Groves, Sergeant 12 W. Howard

1909. Introduction of the Merit or Good Conduct stripe, which was a single inverted stripe worn on the lower right sleeve. In the Herefordshire Constabulary this was limited to fifteen constables with at least 15 years service, and earned an extra increment in pay. The Merit stripe was discontinued just before the second World War.

1911. Permission was given by the Standing Joint Committee for the Chief Constable to purchase one hundred badges for the Special Constabulary. There is no record of whether they were cap or lapel badges, or arm badges (brassards).

1914. Orders were given that enlisted Special Constables were to be issued with arm–bands and a stout stick. There is in existence a brassard bearing the words 'Herefordshire Constabulary Special Constable' which could be the badge referred to in 1911. It was on a leather strap and was intended to be worn with civilian clothes.

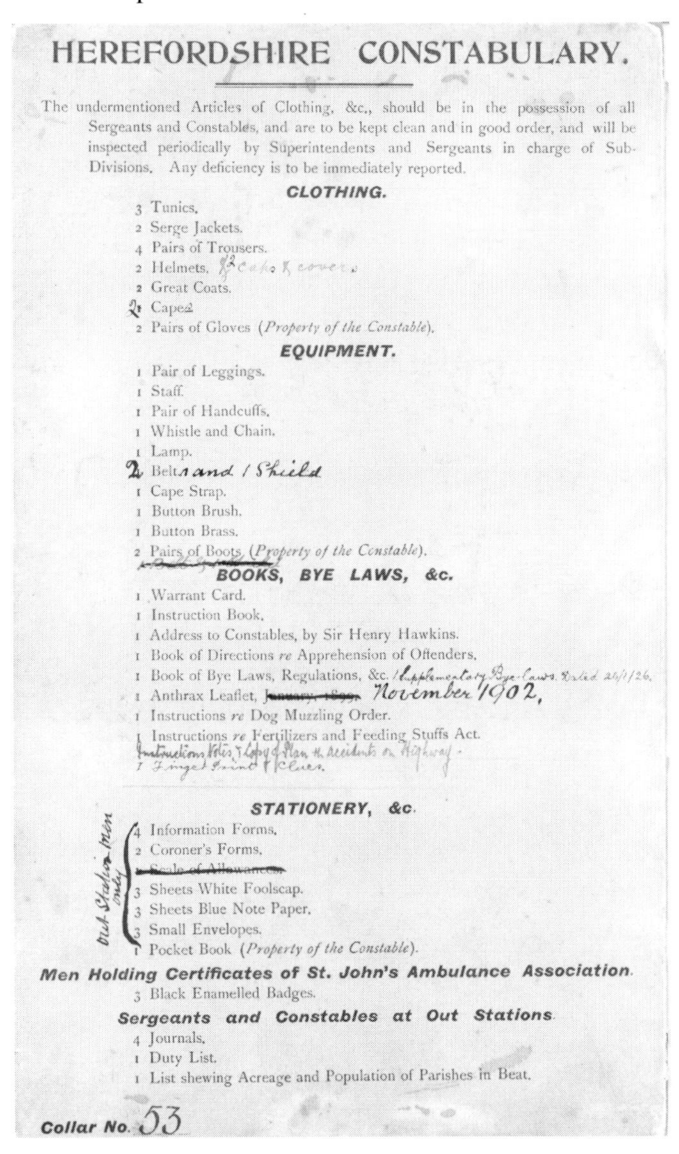

HEREFORDSHIRE CONSTABULARY.

The undermentioned Articles of Clothing, &c., should be in the possession of all Sergeants and Constables, and are to be kept clean and in good order, and will be inspected periodically by Superintendents and Sergeants in charge of Sub-Divisions. Any deficiency is to be immediately reported.

CLOTHING.

3 Tunics.
2 Serge Jackets.
4 Pairs of Trousers.
2 Helmets. & 2 Caps & covers.
2 Great Coats.
2 Capes.
2 Pairs of Gloves (*Property of the Constable*).

EQUIPMENT.

1 Pair of Leggings.
1 Staff.
1 Pair of Handcuffs.
1 Whistle and Chain.
1 Lamp.
2 Belts and 1 Shield
1 Cape Strap.
1 Button Brush.
1 Button Brass.
2 Pairs of Boots (*Property of the Constable*).

BOOKS, BYE LAWS, &c.

1 Warrant Card.
1 Instruction Book.
1 Address to Constables, by Sir Henry Hawkins.
1 Book of Directions *re* Apprehension of Offenders.
1 Book of Bye Laws, Regulations, &c. 1 Supplementary Bye-Laws dated 26/1/26.
1 Anthrax Leaflet, ~~January, 1899,~~ November 1902,
1 Instructions *re* Dog Muzzling Order.
1 Instructions *re* Fertilizers and Feeding Stuffs Act.

STATIONERY, &c.

Out Station men only:
4 Information Forms.
2 Coroner's Forms.
~~Scale of Allowances.~~
3 Sheets White Foolscap.
3 Sheets Blue Note Paper.
3 Small Envelopes.
1 Pocket Book (*Property of the Constable*).

Men Holding Certificates of St. John's Ambulance Association.

3 Black Enamelled Badges.

Sergeants and Constables at Out Stations.

4 Journals.
1 Duty List.
1 List shewing Acreage and Population of Parishes in Beat.

Collar No. 53

This clothing list was issued to PC 53 F.J. Little, on his appointment in 1921. Note 'Collar No. 53' in the bottom left corner. The clothing and equipment card would have been passed on from previous holders of that number, but this practice was discontinued during the service of PC Little.

PC 61 W.W. Weale
stationed at Longtown,
about 1927

1924/5. Constables and Sergeants changed their summer head-gear from the pill-box cap to the peaked cap, with a white cloth cover to be worn during the day. The practice of wearing peaked caps in summer, and helmets in winter continued until the merger in 1967, although helmets were worn all the year round in Hereford City.

Superintendent J. Groves

1925. Superintendent's uniforms were changed, the new outfit consisting of an open-neck tunic, worn with white shirt and tie, with four pockets, four metal buttons and a cloth, attached belt. The pill-box cap was replaced by a peaked cap, with silver braid on the peak and a cloth and wire, Kings crown inside a wreath, cap badge. The badge of rank was a crown over a star on each epaulette.

1928. The helmet design was altered slightly when the metal band was changed to one in patent leather.

It may have been noticed that no mention has so far been made of an Inspector's uniform. The reason being that there was no rank of Inspector in the Herefordshire Constabulary until 1928. Although, just prior to that date, an officer from another Constabulary had been appointed Inspector/Chief Clerk, he did not wear a uniform in that capacity, and was granted £8 per annum clothing allowance.

1928. The rank of Inspector came into being, with the uniform being the same as that of the Superintendent, except that black braid adorned the peak of the cap, and the badge of rank was a single star on the epaulettes.

About 1932. Sergeant's chevrons began to be worn on both sleeves.

1935. A tunic with seven buttons was introduced.

1937. The helmet plate changed from the wreath type with HC scroll, to the Brunswick star with the shield from the Arms of Hereford City in the centre, surmounted by a Tudor (King's) crown. The county of Herefordshire did not have its own Coat of

Arms until one was granted in 1946, therefore part of the City Arms was used on the badge.

1938. The patent leather band on the helmet was changed back to the metal one, and in the same year Superintendent's and Inspector's cap badges were changed to a small star shape with a blue enamel ring and the words 'Herefordshire Constabulary'. There was a shield in the centre, with the Hereford City Arms, and the whole was surmounted by a Tudor crown. The badges of rank were later changed to a Crown for the Superintendent, and either one or two pips for the Inspector.

1939. The First Aid badge was discontinued. By this time the Special Constables were wearing a uniform similar to their regular counterparts, with a cap badge bearing the words 'Herefordshire Special Constabulary'.

It is not quite certain when the rubberised Mackintosh coats and leggings first came into use, but although they were completely waterproof, they caused condensation inside and were not popular. The overcoat, cape and Mackintosh were eventually replaced by a knee-length Gannex coat.

WAPC M.A. Blake
Photographed on 29-6-1942

At the beginning of the second World War, due to the shortage of man-power, women were enlisted into the Women's Auxiliary Police Corps, (WAPC). They were issued with a skirt and open neck tunic, worn with a white shirt and tie, with two breast pockets and an attached belt. The WAPC badge was worn above the left breast pocket. A soft-top peaked cap, with the same badge as that of a constable, was worn.

During the war years small inverted chevrons were worn on the right lower sleeve – one chevron for each year of war service.

After World War Two the first police-women were appointed and wore the same uniform as that of the disbanded WAPC. This uniform continued without change for a number of years, although the caps were changed several times.

Special Constables continued to wear the same type of uniform as their regular counterparts, as did the Police Cadets, who were introduced on 1st. May 1951. The Cadets wore a peaked cap with a blue band , and a shoulder flash with the words 'Police Cadet'. The initial establishment was fixed at five, and the first Cadets to be enrolled were Clifford Davies, stationed at Ross, Richard Jenkins and Graham Hepworth, at Headquarters, and John Sockett at Central Division, followed by Derek Jones at

Leominster, in September.

1951. There was little further change in uniform until 1951 when open-neck tunics, with a blue shirt and black tie were issued. The tunic had two breast pockets and no belt, with numerals worn on the epaulettes. Within a few years the design was changed again to a tunic with four pockets, and an attached cloth belt.

Right,
Cadet W.P. Depper,
who was stationed at Ross.

Left,
PC 127 G. Thwaites,
wearing the new open-neck tunic

1953/4. Following the accession of Queen Elizabeth the Second in 1952 the crown on the badges changed from the Tudor crown to the Edward (Queen's) crown.

1955. It was during the hot summer of 1955 that permission was first granted for tunics to be left off during the day. This was very beneficial to the officer on duty, but as the trousers were not of the self-supporting type, belts of all kinds were worn. Shortly afterwards self-supporting trousers were issued.

1962. Chromium-plated helmet plates and ventilator roses were worn for the first time and the Herefordshire Coat of Arms replaced that of the City on the centre shield of the helmet plate. Chromium cap badges had been worn for some years prior to this.

HEREFORDSHIRE CONSTABULARY
BADGES and INSIGNIA, 1857-1967

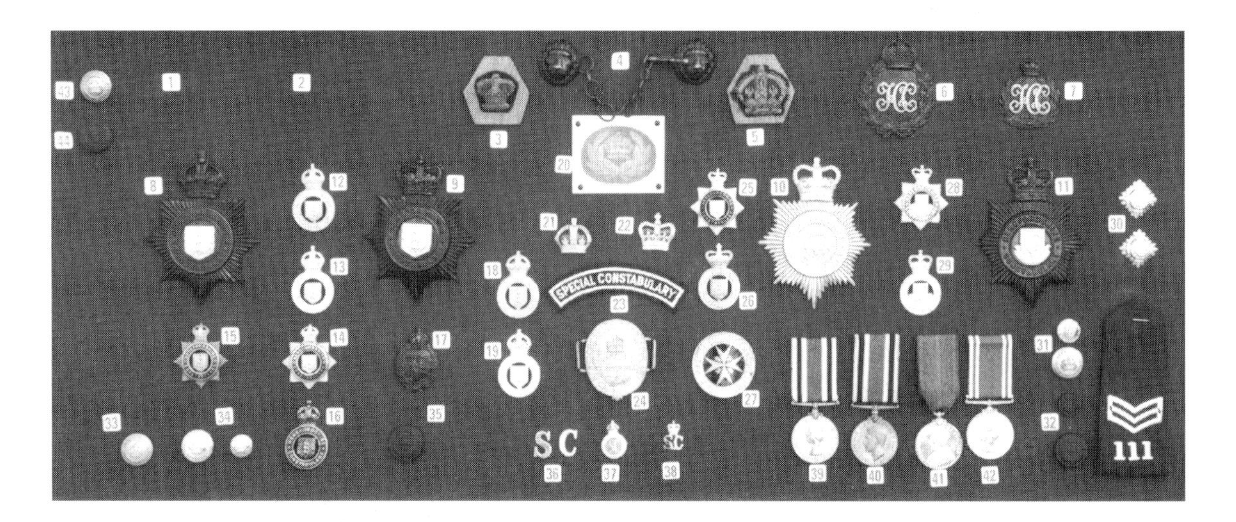

1. Vacant space for Victorian Helmet Plate
2. Vacant space for Victorian Cap Badge.
3. Victorian Officer's Shako Badge.
4. Lion's head Cape Fasteners.
5. King's Crown, Superintendent and Inspector Cap Badge.
6. King's crown Helmet Plate.
7. King's Crown Cap Badge.
8. King's Crown, Star pattern, Helmet Plate, (City of Hereford Arms).
9. Queen's Crown, Star pattern, Helmet Plate, (City of Hereford Arms).
10. Queen's Crown, Star pattern, Chromium Helmet Plate, (Herefordshire Arms).
11. Queen's Crown, Star pattern, Black Helmet Plate, (Herefordshire Arms).
12. King's Crown, White metal Cap Badge.
13. King's Crown, Chromium Cap Badge.
14. King's Crown, Senior Officers, Chromium and Blue Enamel Cap Badge.
15. King's Crown, Senior Officers, Sterling Silver Cap Badge.
16. King's Crown, Black finish Cap Badge.
17. King's Crown, Black finish Cap Badge, with HC scroll and 'Special'.
18. King's Crown, White metal Special Constabulary Cap Badge.
19. King's Crown, Chromium Special Constabulary Cap Badge.
20. Photograph of Superintendent's Wire, Embroidered, Cap Badge.
21. King's Crown, Superintendent's Epaulette Badge of Rank.
22. Queen's Crown, Superintendent's Epaulette Badge of Rank.
23. Special Constabulary Shoulder Flash.
24. Special Constabulary Brassard.
25. Queen's Crown, Senior Officer Cap Badge, (Hereford City Arms).
26. Queen's Crown, Chromium Cap Badge.
27. St. John Ambulance Association First Aid Badge.
28. Queen's Crown, Senior Officer, Cap Badge, (Herefordshire Arms).
29. Queen's Crown, Cap Badge, (Herefordshire Arms).
30. Inspector Badge of Rank, 'Pips'.
31. Queen's Crown, Chromium Buttons.
32. Queen's Crown, Black Buttons.
33. King's Crown, White Metal Button.
34. King's Crown, Chromium Buttons.
35. King's Crown, Black Button.
36. Special Constabulary Collar or Epaulette Letters.
37. Special Constabulary Lapel Badge, Civilian clothes.
38. Special Constabulary Lapel Badge
39. Queen Elizabeth the Second, Special Constabulary Long Service Medal.
40. King George the Sixth, Special Constabulary Long Service Medal.
41. King George the Fifth, Sterling Silver, Police Issue Commemorative Coronation Medal.
42. Queen Elizabeth the Second, Police Long Service and Good Conduct Medal.
43. Victorian Crown, White Metal Button.
44. Victorian Crown, Black finish Button.

Extra item: Sergeant's Epaulette, Bottom right.

HEREFORDSHIRE CONSTABULARY

Helmet plates and Cap badges – slightly less than actual size.

These two recent photographs show, above, the almost unchanged façade of the Herefordshire Constabulary Headquarters, built in the late 1890's, to replace the rooms under the Shire Hall, Hereford, which had been used since the formation of the Constabulary in 1857. The picture below shows the present, smartened, state of the building in St. John Street, Hereford, which was leased in 1939, and used as Headquarters throughout the war years, but was found to be unsuitable. It was vacated in 1947, when the move to 'Brockington' took place.

BROMYARD DIVISION,1876.

From L. to R., PCs 40 G. Harding, 47 H. Neale, Sgt. 3 R. Strangward, PC 29 G. Hill, Supt. T. Ovens, Sgt.44 J. Smith, PCs 42 H. Baynham, 31 W. Williams

LEOMINSTER DIVISION, 1882
From L. to R., Supt. T. Dykes, PCs. 43 H. Woodyatt, 21 A. Prothero, 14 T. Marston, 37 G. Bluck, 45 T. Lewis, Sgt. 5 J. Baynham
This photograph of Superintendent Dykes, taken in the year of his retirement, and the one earlier in the book of Robert Dallow, are the only two pictures of former Superintendent Constables.
Thomas Dykes was a native of Nantwich, Cheshire, and after six years as a soldier, served for five years in the Lancashire Constabulary, before becoming a Superintendent Constable at Weobley for four years. He was one of the original Superintendents in the Herefordshire Constabulary, stationed at Harewood End.
He died in Hereford in 1902.

Above, L: The earliest known photograph of a Herefordshire Constable, PC 32 J. Lewis, who joined on 27-3-1860, and served in Weobley, Whitney, Harewood End and Abbeydore Divisions before his resignation on 16-1-1864.
Above, R: PC 14 T. Marston, c.1880, who joined 22-3-1879, retired on 1-7-1911, as a Superintendent.
Below: L: PC 61 J. Lewis, c.1878, joined on 25-3-1878, and died whilst serving, on 1-4-1896.
Centre: PC 43 H. Warrington. During his police service he was stationed at Ashperton, Ross, Bodenham and Mansel Lacy and retired in 1892. He was the great-grandfather of PC 165 P.S. Warrington
Below,R: PC 34 J. Haynes, c.1873, was appointed 20-1-1873, resigned 1-6-1875, rejoined 15-9-1875, resigned again 1-10-1896. Joined for the third time, as PC 17, 1-2-1897, and finally pensioned 1-10-1897.

YEOMANRY CAMP, c.1885
L. to R: Sgt. 5 J. Baynham, PCs. 43 H. Woodyatt, 24 G.Williams, 8 T. Wright

Below, Left: Supt. W. Cope, Worcestershire Constabulary, with his father, Supt. W. Cope, Herefordshire Constabulary, c.1890.

Right: PC 29 B. Vearnalls, c.1890, served from 10-8-1882 to 16-1-1909.

HEREFORD and ABBEYDORE DIVISION, 1889,
including WHITNEY SECTION.
Back row, L. to R: PCs. 21 A Protheroe, 40 G. Hall, 26 R.W. Edwards, 15 G. Gayden.
Middle row, L. to R: PCs 11 J.F. Morris, 41 J Greenhouse, 55 C.W. Phelps, Sgt. 25 R. Lewis,
PCs. 9 A. Barnett, 29 B. Vearnalls, 35 G. Lee, Sgt. 49 J. Phillips, PCs 3 W.J. Evans,
10 E. Rogers, 47 J.E. Price.
Front row, L. to R: seated: Sergeant 19 S. Price, Superintendent W. Cope.

Below: PC 1 W.T. Hadley, c.1895, on patrol in the village of Eardisley, where he was stationed from 1891 to 1907, before his move to Shobdon. He joined Herefordshire Constabulary in July 1885, after a short period of service in Kidderminster Borough Police. He retired in 1912.

LEOMINSTER and WIGMORE DIVISION, 1893
Back row, L. to R: PCs 16 J. Jones, 13 W.J. Powell, 32 A. Biggs, 45 A.J. Oakley,
Middle row, L. to R: PCs 41 J. Greenhouse, 7 A.J. Jeans, 2 W. Thomas, 9 A. Barnett, 60 B. Hackett, 3 A.D. Titcombe,
Front row, L. to R: Sgts. 53 J. Smith, 23 W. Jones, Supt. R. Strangward, Sgts. 54 A. Hyde, 14 T. Marston

RICHARD STRANGWARD.

Richard Strangward was born at Shobdon, Herefordshire, in 1844, and in his youth went to Crewe where he became a fireman on the London and North Western Railway. Wishing to see something of the world he travelled to New York in 1861, on the second trip of the Great Eastern. The Civil War had begun, and after about two years Richard Strangward enlisted in the Northern Army. He was not involved in any major battles, but happened to be in Ford's Theatre, Washington on the night that Abraham Lincoln was shot by John Wilkes Booth, and was one of the group who found the assassin, in hiding, after a nine day search. After six years in America he returned to England and was appointed PC 3 in the Herefordshire Constabulary, on 7-6-1867. After short periods of service in Pembridge and Ledbury, he moved to Ross in 1868, where he earned himself the name of 'Deerhound' because of his skill in following and capturing wanted persons. His ability was noticed and he was promoted Sergeant, and moved to Bromyard in 1875, then to Cradley in 1881. His promotion to Superintendent came in 1882, together with a move to Leominster, where he remained until 1895. During his service at Leominster he was involved in several incidents which added to the unusual character of his life. In 1889 he was struck by lightning at Kingsland, which incident necessitated his absence from duty for three weeks. In 1890 the Leominster fire-brigade was called to a fire at Eardisland, and because of a delay in finding sufficient harness for the horses, the driver, evidently trying to make up lost time, allowed the engine to over-run the horses, resulting in most of the crew, including Mr. Strangward, being thrown off, the driver being buried in a ditch of mud and slush. The rest of the crew were eventually located by the use of matches and a borrowed lantern, and when the horses were finally recaptured, the uninjured members of the crew arrived at the scene of the fire just as it was doused by villagers. Supt. Strangward's last move was to Weobley, from where he retired in 1899, to live in Leominster until his death in 1910. He was buried in the church-yard at Kingsland, with bearers at the funeral being, PS 35 Lee, PS 64 Weaver, PC 1 Hadley, PC 28 Wright.

PARADE AT HEREFORD, 1895.

(Possibly on the occasion of the retirement of Captain Telfer)

Back row, L. to R: PCs 65 T. Baugh, 11 J. F. Morris, 9 A. Barnett, 57 A. Clee, 28 T. Wright, 66 S.Williams,70 W. Wall, 71 J.K. Jones,

Middle row, L. to R: PCs 67 D. Thomas, 55 J. Carver, 45 A. Oakley, 13 W.J. Powell, 49 G. Preece, 64 A Weaver, 20 W.W. Jones, 59 J.S. Walker, 16 H.E. King, New recruit (in civvies).

Front row, L. to R: PCs 38 J. Boucher, 50 J. Powell, 15 G. Gayden, Sgt. 24 G. Williams, Supt. G. Smith, Sgt. 40 G. Hall, Sgt. 62 T. McNaught, PCs 10 E. Rogers, 35 G. Lee.

Below:

BROMYARD DIVISION, 1896

Back row, L. to R., PCs 67 D. Thomas, 16 H.E. King, 11 J.F. Morris, 6 W. Thomas, 17 J. Cross 32 A. Biggs, 51 W.H. Trigg

Front row, L. to R., Sergeant 4 I.J. Lloyd, Superintendent R. Lewis, Sergeant 63 C. Rooke

(The boy in front is a son of Supt.Lewis, Herbert, who was killed during the first World War).

THOMAS OVENS

Thomas Ovens was appointed PC 39 on 16-9-1863, the first of four brothers to join the Herefordshire Constabulary, and the beginning of a tradition of police service in the Ovens family. His son, Charles, joined Gloucestershire Constabulary in 1886, transferring to Hereford City Police in 1888, where he became Chief Inspector. Thomas Ovens rose through the ranks, and after several moves, became Superintendent at Bromyard, on 7-8-1875.
He retired from Bromyard on 16-10-1891, and died at Ocle Pychard on 5-2-1918.

Below, L. to R:
PC 39 J. Evans and PC 55 C.W. Phelps, c.1890

John Evans was appointed on 20-10-1888, and died whilst serving at Whitchurch, on 22-2-1896, leaving a widow and one child.
Charles W. Phelps joined on 1-12-1887, and resigned whilst serving at Leominster, on 19-9-1891.

PC 17 A. Lawrence,
joined the Constabulary in August 1900, and ended his service at Stretton Sugwas in November 1929.

LEOMINSTER and WIGMORE DIVISION, 1896.
Back row, L. to R: PCs 33 H. Barber, 46 J.H. Williams, 45 A. Oakley, 72 J. Evans,
Middle row, L. to R.: PCs 41 J. Greenhouse, 18 W. Brookes, 57 A. Clee, 60 B. Hackett, 13 W.J. Powell,
Front row, L. to R.: Sgt. 26 R.W. Edwards, Supt. G. Ovens, Sgt. 2 W.Thomas, Sgt. 21 A. Protheroe.
George Ovens, a brother of Thomas Ovens, was appointed PC 37 on 10-6-1868. He retired on 16-7-1899, and died at Weobley on 19-6-1906

Below:
KINGTON SECTION, 1897.
Back row, L. to R: PCs 47 T. Williams, 22 T. Hyde, 54 J. Broad, 28 T. Wright.
Front row, L. to R: Sergeant 19 S. Price, PC 1 W.T. Hadley

LEOMINSTER and WIGMORE DIVISION, 1899.

Back row, L. to R.: PCs 39 C. Lane, 61 W. Weaver, 49 G. Preece, 33 H. Barber, 70 W. Wall,
Middle row, L. to R: PCs 18 W. Brookes, 13 W.J. Powell, 26 R.W. Edwards, 46 J.H. Williams,
17 S. Taylor, 57 A. Clee
Seated, L. to R: Sgts. 65 T. Baugh, 14 T. Marston, Supt. G. Ovens, Sgts. 21 A. Protheroe, 35 G. Lee
Unknown boy

Below:
L: PC 61 J. Lewis, a different uniform to his earlier picture, and wearing a white stock.
R: Sergeant 14 T. Marston, soon after his promotion in 1891. He became Superintendent on 1-9-1899

ROSS DIVISION, TOWN and RURAL, 1899.
Standing, L. to R: PCs 4 I.J. Lloyd, 66 S. Williams, 3 A. D. Titcombe, 69 C Kendal, 56 H.J. Luckett, 36 L. Lewis, 72 S. Wynn
Seated, L. to R: Sergeant 9 A. Barnett, Superintendent A.T. Cope.

Below, Left: PS 63 C. Rooke and PC 39 C. Lane, c.1901
Right: PC 30 W. Davies, c.1902, *'May I have your name, please, Sir?'*

BETWEEN APRIL and OCTOBER, 1904.

Back row, L. to R: PCs 45 A.J. Oakley, 54 J. Broad, 46 J.H. Williams, 59 J.S. Walker, 19 W.T. Tomkins, 51 T. Goode, 13 T. Roberts, 43 A.G. Tompkins.

Middle row, L. to R: PCs 73 G. Hall, 44 J. Gunter, 5 R. Edwards, 67 D. Thomas, Sgt. 69 C. Kendal, PCs 60 B. Hackett, 40 D. Evans, 23 J. Evans.

Front row, L. to R: PCs 3 A.D. Titcombe, 7 J.. Jeans, 29 B. Vearnalls, Sgt. 4 I.J. Lloyd, Supt. A.T. Cope, Sgt. 65 T. Baugh, PCs 64 A. Weaver, 1 W.T. Hadley.

A formidable body of men drawn from stations throughout the county, and commanded by the Hereford Superintendent. It is not known what the occasion was, but the photograph is unique, in that it is the earliest showing that style of overcoat, and the only one where the men are wearing leather gaiters.

Below, c.1905

PC 29 B. Vearnalls communing with some of the locals, outside the Five Bridges Inn, Much Cowarne.

WINFORTON, 1904.

PC 1 W.T. Hadley surveying one of the damaged vehicles at the scene of the first recorded multi-vehicle road accident in the county. The picture below shows the scene, with the two cars still *in situ*, and some of the by-standers who had come out to view, including Mrs. Eliza Hadley with her two daughters, Frances and Edith, on the left. The accident occurred at Winforton in 1904, between a Darracq motor-car, EU 40, and an Argyle chauffeur-driven car, which was carrying the Duke of Connaught to a review of troops at Brecon. Fortunately the Duke travelled with a back-up vehicle in attendance, and was able to continue his journey. The driver of EU40 eventually appeared before Bredwardine Justices, charged with certain offences, one of which related to drink.

William T. Hadley was the first of four generations of the family to join the police service. He was born at Ullingswick, and initially joined the Kidderminster Borough Police. After a short period of service there he joined the Herefordshire Constabulary in 1885, and served at Lyonshall, Eardisley and Shobdon until his retirement in 1912. He continued to live at Shobdon until his death in 1943.

BRAMPTON BRYAN HORSE FAIR, c.1906
PC 64 A. Weaver and Sergeant 2 W. Thomas

Below:
Superintendent S. Price, pre-1908, in his immaculate turn-out, photographed in the yard at the rear of Leominster Police Station, Burgess Street.
The carts were supplied to Superintendents, together with an allowance to provide a horse.
Stephen Price joined the Constabulary in 1878, after a career in the army, much of which was spent in India. He was a 1st. Class Sergeant within 6 years, and became a Superintendent in 1898.

PC 43 A.G. Tompkins, c.1903
Served from 7-5-1900 to 30-6-1930

PC 39 C. Lane, c.1906, served in the
Constabulary from 22-6-1896 until 1-6-1911

Below:
The village street at Shobdon, in 1908. PC 1 W.T. Hadley, with daughter Edith, standing outside the police station, on the right. The building on the left is the Post Office, and the man in the centre with the wheel, is probably one of the Clifton family, the village blacksmiths.

MUCH COWARNE, 1909.
PC 29 B. Vearnalls moved from Bishop's Frome to Much Cowarne in 1904,
where he is pictured taking refreshment with the hop-pickers.
Below:
Left: Superintendent W. Thomas, c.1910. Served 16-5-1883 to 20-1-1916
Right: PC 14 F.W. Knight, c.1905. After fourteen years service he died from Rheumatic Fever in 1919.

PC 53 R. Preece, c.1906, served in
the Constabulary from 14-8-1905
until 1-10-1920.

Above, right:
PC 10 W.J. Brown, c.1910.
Served from 1-5-1908, retiring in February
1935 with the rank of Sergeant.
During the Second World War he re-joined as
a First Reserve Sergeant.
He was the grand-father of
PC 46 R.G. Brown,
of Herefordshire Constabulary.

Right:
HAREWOOD END SECTION, c.1909.

Standing, L. to R.: PC 68 G.F. Yapp,
PC 57 G. Davies, PC 24 G.T. Brierley.
Seated: Sergeant 38 J. Boucher
PC 66 S. Williams.

PARADE AT ROSS, c.1900.
A contingent of four
Herefordshire Constabulary
Officers, led by a Sergeant.
Occasion unknown.

The banner bears the Arms of
Hereford City and the mace-
bearers would have been
Hereford City Police officers.

FIRST AID COMPETITION, c.1914.
Photograph taken at Ross
railway station.

Herefordshire Constabulary
represented by, L. to R.,
PC 63 E. Everett,
PC 74 C.E. Greenway,
PC 59 T.J. Morgan.

FIRE AT EASTNOR, 1910.

L. to R: PC 40 D. Evans
PC 14 F.W. Knight

PC Evans served in the
Herefordshire Constabulary for
two months in 1899, before being
recalled to the Colours. He
returned in October 1900, and was
again recalled to the
Grenadier Guards until 1902.
His final period of service from
1-9-1902 was again interrupted
when he was seconded as a Drill
Sergeant in 1914. He retired on
pension in 1926.

ROSS DIVISION, 1909.

Back Row, L. to R: PCs 29 J.M. Kelly, 39 C. Lane, 68 G.F. Yapp, 19 W.T. Tomkins, 63 H.J. Thomas, 24 G.T.Brierley, 57 G. Davies, 43 A.G. Tompkins, 49 G. Preece.
Front row, L. to R: PC 66 S.Williams, Sgt. 38 J. Boucher, Supt. T. Marston, Sgt. 3 A.D. Titcombe, PC 6 W. Thomas.

L. to R:
Sgt. 9 A. Barnett, PC 37 W. Proctor, PC 5 R. Edwards, c.1909.

Sergeant 64 A.Weaver with Sir J. Rankin, MP, at Kingsland and District Flower Show, c.1910.

Below, right:RICHARD LEWIS, joined Herefordshire Constabulary in 1867, and was promoted Sergeant in 1879. He became Superintendent at Bromyard in 1891 and retired there in January 1910. From 1920 until his death in 1925 he sat on the Magistrate's bench at Bromyard.
One of his sons, Leonard Lewis, was Superintendent/Chief Clerk at Hereford.

PC 11 J.F.MORRIS.
PC Morris was stationed at Kingstone
when he retired, in 1909, after 24 years service.

RICHARD LEWIS

FIRST AEROPLANE TO LAND AT ROSS, 1912.

L. to R: in uniform,
PCs 49 G. Preece, 51 A. Davies, 68 G.F. Yapp, Sgt. 59 J.S. Walker, Supt. J. Broad,
PCs 7 J. Jeans, 30 W. Davies, 58 B.C. Hardwick.

The lady and three children are the wife and family of Superintendent Broad.

Above, L. to R: PCs 47 W.J. Griffin and 21 W.E. Holl, at Ledbury, c.1912.
Below, L. to R: PC 66 H. Powell, c.1913, PC 79 S. Painter, c.1914.
PC Painter was the father of Geoffrey Painter, Chief Inspector in the Herefordshire Constabulary at the merger in 1967, who, after service in Worcestershire, returned to Hereford as Chief Superintendent.

WEOBLEY SECTION, c. 1903.
Rear, L. to R: PCs 45 A. J. Oakley, 19 W.T. Tomkins, 14 G. Reade, 16 H.E. King.
Front, L. to R: PC 60 B. Hackett, Sgt. 8 J. Groves, Supt. T. Marston, Sgt. 28 T. Wright, PC 1 W.T. Hadley

Left: PC 1 C.F. Harris was posted to Bishop's Frome after his WW1 army service, and remained there for twenty-seven years, proving each year, at hop-picking time, that he was the right man in the right place.
Right: PC 78 T. Ovens was grandson of Supt. T. Ovens, son of C.G. Ovens, of Hereford City Police, and father of Michael and Neville Ovens. He joined the Constabulary in 1914, and served till 1946.

Above, L: PC 77 E.D.H. Walters, returned as PC 28 after war service. R: On the left, PC 56 J. Thomas, who joined the Constabulary in November 1913, was recalled to the Army in August 1914, and died of wounds received in action. On the right: PC 63 E. Everett who served from July 1913 to July 1939. Below, L: PC 58 W.A. Barrell. He joined the Constabulary in January 1913, enlisted in May 1915, and was killed in action 11-2-1917. R: PC 32 A.T. Bullock, served in the Royal Garrison Artillery.

Left to Right: Superintendent C. Rooke, Superintendent J. Groves, Superintendent J.H. Williams.

Charles Rooke joined the Herefordshire Constabulary in 1883, resigning in May 1885. The following month he joined the Leominster Borough Police, and after the amalgamation of 1889 became PC 63 in the Herefordshire Constabulary. He was promoted Sergeant in 1895, and became Superintendent at Leominster in 1908, where he remained until his retirement in 1921.

James Groves was appointed PC 8 on 11-11-1889, and became Sergeant in 1897. He ended his police career as Superintendent at Leominster, following Superintendent Rooke, and retired in January 1925.

J.H. Williams, pictured here in 1921, joined Herefordshire Constabulary as PC 46 in October 1892 and was promoted to Sergeant at Bromyard in 1905. He became Superintendent at Ledbury in 1911, where he remained until his retirement in 1923.
He died in March 1940 and is buried at Blakemere.

Below: Sergeant 31 H. Wright, pictured here with a group of the staff at Holmer Hall, c.1920, served in the Constabulary from September 1896 until October 1931.

VISIT OF H.M.I. TO HEADQUARTERS AND HEREFORD DIVISION, SEPTEMBER 1921.

Back row, L. to R: PCs 19 A.C.J. Edwards, 79 S. Painter, 13 T. Theakstone, 33 W.H. Nash.
Middle row, L. to R: PC 75 T. Barwell, Sgt. 55 J. Carver, PCs17 A. Lawrence, 28 E.D.H. Walters, 15 F. Shakesheff, Sgt 42 H.W. Williams.
Front row, L. to R: Superintendent L. Lewis, (Chief Clerk), His Majesty's Inspector of Constabulary, Sir Leonard Dunning, Chief Constable, Captain E.T.S. Stanhope, Deputy Chief Constable, Superintendent A. Weaver.

LEOMINSTER DIVISION, 1921.

Back row, L. to R: PCs 23 H.Arrowsmith, 56 R.J. Broben, 76 R. Baugh.
Middle row, L. to R: PCs 57 J. Greenway, 74 H.H. Marston, 32 A.T. Bullock, 27 E.S. Edwards, 54 A. Miles, 39 L. James, 58 B.C. Hardwick.
Front row, L. to R: PC 77 G.W. Powell, Sgt. 34 C.H. Matthews, Sgt. 50 W.F. Powell, Supt. C. Rooke, Sgt. 31 H. Wright, PC 30 W. Davies.

His Majesty's Inspector, Sir Leonard Dunning,
Chief Constable, Captain E.T.S. Stanhope,
Deputy Chief Constable, Superintendent A. Weaver, in 1921.

Below: PC 35 J. J. Chance, joined the Constabulary after service in WW1, and during his twenty-seven years service was stationed at Bromyard, Leominster, Bredwardine and Pontrilas.

Above: Superintendent J. Broad and Sergeant 3 A.D. Titcombe.

Superintendent Broad joined as PC 54 in 1896 and retired in 1927.

Sergeant Titcombe completed thirty-one years service in 1921.

Right: PC 26 J.H. Francis, who joined the Constabulary in 1901, was reputed to be one of the heaviest police officers in England.

HEREFORD, SHIREHALL, 1922.
Parade in honour of Superintendent L. Lewis, on his retirement.
(Superintendent Lewis attended a presentation which was made to him,
but was unable to be present at the parade, due to his ill-health.)
Back row, L. to R., PCs 13 W.J. Lines, 38 C.H. Davies, 66 H. Powell, 21 C. Powell, 74 H.H. Marston,
15 F. Shakesheff, 53 F.J. Little, 36 G.E. Meredith, 76 R. Baugh, 46 J. Prosser, 49 H.C. Bowery,
58 B.C. Hardwick, 6 A. Lewis.

Middle row, L. to R., PCs 2 A.H. Moss, 14 A. Moss, 27 E.S. Edwards, 28 E.D.H. Walters, 79 S. Painter,
16 F. Hales, 40 D. Evans, 59 T.J. Morgan, 75 T. Barwell, 62 T. Hayward, 23 H. Arrowsmith.

Front row,L. to R., PC 60 T.B Wheeler, PS 24 G.T. Brierley, Superintendents J.H. Williams, J. Groves,
A. Weaver, J. Broad, PS 42 H.W. Williams, PC 17 A. Lawrence.

THE OPENING OF THE BRIDGE AT LITTLE HEREFORD, 1925.
L. to R., PCs39 L. James, 30 W. Davies, Supt. G.T. Brierley, Sgt. 25 J. Edge,
PCs 47 W.J. Griffin, 41 E. Jarrett, 49 H.C. Bowery, 71 A.F. Rock.

LEDBURY DIVISION, photographed at Bromyard Police Station, 1923
Back row, L. to R., PCs 11 W.E. Thomas, 20 S.G. Whittaker, 65 G. Williams, 29 A. Hopkins, 78 T. Ovens.
Middle row, L. to R., PCs 64 D. Morris, 9 A.R. Smith, 80 L.J. Jones, 1 C.F. Harris, 7 T. Dix, 35 J. Chance.
Front row, L. to R., PC 18 H.V. Campion, Sgt. 4 W.C. Gwynn, Sgt. 12 W. Howard, Supt. J.H. Williams, Sgt. 72 S. Wynn, PCs 45 A.J. Oakley, 47 W.J. Griffin.

Above, left: Chief Constable H.F.M. Munro, on the right, wearing the uniform of the Royal Irish Constabulary, in company with Chief Constable T. Rawson, of Hereford City Police, in the funeral procession of Police/Fireman Reginald Stephens, of Hereford City Police, in 1924.
Above, right: Sergeant 24 G.T. Brierley, c.1920. He was promoted to Superintendent in 1923, and was Deputy Chief Constable from 1934 until his retirement in 1945, after nearly forty-one years service.

LEOMINSTER DIVISION, 1925, (wearing summer uniform, peaked cap).
Back row, L. to R.: PC s. 48 J.J. White, 3 C.R. Moody, 71 A.F. Rock, 36 G.E. Meredith, 53 F.J. Little, 16 F. Hales.
Middle row, L. to R: PCs. 14 A. Moss, 27 E.S. Edwards, 39 L. James, 37 R.G. Pugh, 57 J. Greenway, 70 T. Williams, 35, J. J. Chance, 30 W. Davies, 49 H.C. Bowery, 47 W.J. Griffin, 54 A. Miles, 41 E. Jarrett, 73 H.D. Main, 6 A. Lewis, 46 J. Prosser, 23 H. Arrowsmith.
Front row, L. to R: Sgts. 32 A.T. Bullock, 25 J. Edge, 34 C.H. Matthews, Supt. J. Groves, Sgt. 68 G. Yapp, PCs 51 A. Davies, 43 A.G. Tompkins.

Below, Right: On the right, c.1924, PC 76 H.E.J. Penry, of Herefordshire Constabulary, with his father PC 8 G. Penry of Hereford City Police.
Below, Left: Sergeant 5 R. Edwards, who joined the Constabulary on 1-11-1901. He died suddenly whilst investigating a house-breaking at Haywood, Hereford on 20-3-1928.

Three new recruits.
Standing, L. to R: PC 37 A.E. Matthews and
PC 40 J.E.Keyte, who were both appointed on 1-5-1926.
Seated: PC 45 J.R.Cole, who was appointed on 1-12-1925,
and left after two years to join the Malay States Police.

Below: PC 22 T. Green, who was a native of Gloucestershire, joined the Constabulary in 1907, and was stationed at Leominster and Weobley, then St. Weonards, where he remained for eleven years. He moved to Walford for the rest of his service, and continued to live in that area following his retirement in 1935.

Above: PC 8 J. Bayliss.
PC Bayliss joined the Constabulary in 1911 and saw service with Bristol Heavy Artillery, during WW1. After his return to police service, he was eventually posted to Stretton Sugwas in 1929, where he remained until his retirement in 1946. He was the first occupant of the new Police Station, in 1934.

Below: PC 23 H. Arrowsmith, with his own Morgan car, at Norton Canon.

L. to R: Sergeant 5 R. Edwards, PCs 37 A.E. Matthews,
45 J.R. Cole and 40 J.E. Keyte, about 1926

Above, right: Sergeant 28 E.D.H. Walters, who became Superintendent at Leominster, in 1941.

Below, left: PC 29 A. Hopkins, who joined the Constabulary in 1914, served in the army from 1915 to 1918, and was posted to Bredenbury when he re-joined. After twelve years at that station he moved to Pembridge, until his retirement in 1950.

Below, right: PC 64 D. Morris, joined the Constabulary in 1914, and served in the army during WW1. In 1921 he was posted to Burley Gate where he remained until 1927 when he was posted to Shobdon. He retired there in 1943.

Above, Left: PC 21 C. Powell. Right: PC 35 J.J. Chance and PC 39 L James, at the Iron Cross, Leominster. PC James was the grandfather of former Detective Constable Granville Smith, of West Mercia Constabulary.

Below, Left: PC 9 A.R. Smith. Joined in 1914, after ten years service in the Royal Navy – hence his nickname 'Gun-boat'. On re-call to the Navy in WW1 he served on HMS Ocean which was sunk by a mine in the Dardanelles, and was later on HMS Monitor when it blew up. He was present at the surrender of the German Fleet, and was mentioned in despatches.

Below, Right: PC 36 G.E. Meredith, served from 1919 to 1945.

Above, left: PC 61 E.C.Wills, at Kington. Right: PC 88 C. E. Dominey, at Ross

Below, left: Sergeant 73 H.D. Main and PC 9 A.R. Smith. Right: PC 6 A. Lewis

LEDBURY SECTION, 1928
Back row, L. to R: PCs 11 W.E. Thomas, 78 T. Ovens, 48 J.J. White, 7 T. Dix, 63 E. Everett.
Front row, L. to R: PC 18 H.V. Campion, Sergeant 4 W.C.Gwynn, 77 G.W. Powell.

L. to R: Superintendent J. Edge, PC 64 D. Morris and Sergeant 23 H. Arrowsmith, in 1935.

PARADE AT HEREFORD, 1928.
OUTSIDE SHIRE HALL HEADQUARTERS.

Back row, in civilian clothing, L. to R: F.A. Jackson, K.C. Weaver.

Third row, L. to R: PCs 63 E. Everett, 48 J.J. White, 5 J. Cole, 24 M.A. Barter, 11 W.E. Thomas, 53 F.J. Little, 76 H.J. Penry, 17 A. Lawrence, 54 A. Miles, 75 T. Barwell, 6 A. Lewis, 64 D. Morris, 30 E.E. Bendall, 45 G. Christopher, 56 R.J. Broben.

Second row, L. to R: PS 79 S. Painter, PCs 3 C.R. Moody, 59 T.J. Morgan, 49 H.C. Bowery, 74 H.H.. Marston, 21 C. Powell, 80 L.J. Jones, 9 A.R. Smith, 70 E.R.P. Watkins, 33 W.H. Nash, 62 T. Hayward, 22 T. Green, 40 J.E. Keyte, 36 G.E. Meredith, 50 W.F. Powell, 7 T. Dix, 69 T. Craig, 65 G. Williams, 39 L. James, 13 W.J. Lines, 46 J. Prosser, 42 H.W. Williams, 8 J. Bayliss.

Front row, seated, L. to R: PC 51 A. Davies, Sergeants 32 A.T. Bullock, 4 W.C. Gwynn, 68 G. Yapp, 31 H. Wright, Inspector J. Edge, Superintendent G.T. Brierley, Chief Constable H.F.M. Munro, Superintendent and Deputy Chief Constable A. Weaver, Superintendent W.J. Hutchinson, Sergeants 67 D. Thomas, 60 T.B. Wheeler, 10 W.J. Brown, 28 E.D.H. Walters, 78 T. Ovens.

LEDBURY SECTION, 1933
Back row, L. to R: PCs 48 J.J. White, 40 J. E. Keyte, 31 J.R. Bayley, 71 A. Rock, 11 W.E. Thomas.
Seated: Sergeant 28 E.D.H.Walters, Superintendent A.Weaver, PC 18 H.V. Campion

Left: PCs 15 F. Shakesheff and 34 D. Grigg. PC Shakesheff joined the Constabulary in 1919, after service in the Herefordshire Regiment during WW1. He spent 16 years of his service at Cradley, retiring in 1938.
Right: PC 25 W.R. Wakefield who served with the Grenadier Guards before joining the Constabulary, was recalled for army service in December 1939. He became a Warrant Officer in the Corps of Military Police, and was awarded a Certificate of Merit by General Montgomery for outstanding good service.
He was honoured with the MBE, in 1945, in recognition of gallant and distinguished army service in north-west Europe.

Above, Left: Sergeant 53 F.J. Little, on promotion to Sergeant in 1935.

Above, Right: Sergeant 6 A. Lewis, joined the Constabulary in 1919, following service in Europe with the Royal Horse Artillery. During his army service he was in action many times, including the battles of the Somme and Longueville, and was awarded the Military Medal and Bar. He retired from the police service in 1958. From his early days as a groom he maintained an interest in horses throughout his life.

Below, L: Sergeant 20 S.G. Whittaker, just before his promotion to Inspector in 1934. He remained at Ross as Inspector until his retirement in 1947. He was a keen sportsman throughout his service.
R: Sergeant 23 H Arrowsmith, joined the Constabulary in 1919, after service with the Grenadier Guards. He served in various parts of the county, ending his service as Sergeant at Weobley.

Above: PC 72 T. Rees, on duty at the Three Counties Show, in 1934, during the visit of Their Royal Highnesses, The Duke and Duchess of York.

Right: PC 75 T.A. Barwell guarding the trophies at the North Hereford Hunt Point-to-Point, in 1937. PC Barwell re-joined the Constabulary in 1939, as a First Police Reserve, and worked the Bodenham beat.

Forty-nine Police Officers leading the funeral cortege of former Superintendent J. Groves, at Leominster, 1936.

Above, Left: PC 43 G.W. Barker. Right: Parade at Leominster, c.1930, led by, on the left, Supt. G.T. Brierley, centre, Sgt. 79 S. Painter, right, Inspector J. Edge.

Below, Left: on the left, PC 18 H.V. Campion, PC 31 J.R. Bayley.
Right: PC 74 H.H. Marston, son of former Superintendent T. Marston.

PC 34 D. Grigg

As an Inspector under the Diseases of Animals Act part of the duties was to supervise the dipping of sheep.

Above, L. to R: PC 18 H.V. Campion and PC 25 A.H. Rushton.
Unfortunately PC Rushton lost his life, in a road traffic accident, whilst off duty, in Hereford, in 1933 .
PC Campion joined in 1900, retired in 1935, having spent the last twenty years of his service at Bosbury.

PC 87 W.J. Williams, was well-known in the Canon Pyon area, and ended his police service at Dilwyn.

Left: PC 74 H.H. Marston, 'being led by a mystic power?' at Leominster.

Above, Left: PC 42 J.A. Kelly. Right: Sgt. 34 D. Grigg and PC 84 C.H. Lappage, at Ross.

Below, Left: PC 72 T. Rees, who joined the Constabulary in 1928, served as Sergeant at Kington and was promoted to Inspector in 1958. In 1959 he became Superintendent at Leominster, then at the merger in 1967 was appointed deputy to Chief Superintendent C.W. Wallin, in charge of 'E' Division. He is very well-known in County bowling circles.

Right: PC 45 G. Christopher, retired as an Inspector at Hereford.

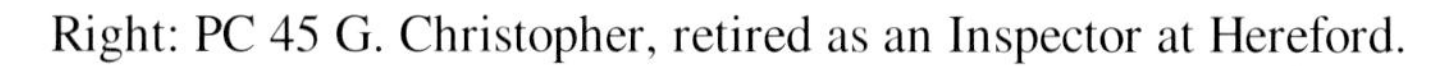

HEREFORD DIVISION, H.M.I. PARADE, JUNE 1938.

Back row, L. to R: PCs 43 G. W. Barker, 60 D.C. Stacey, 52 G.W.H. Hill, 47 W. Franzen, 18 F.G. Stephens, 67 F.J. Griffin, 81 D.A. Gibson, 5 J. Cole, 34 D. Grigg.

Middle row, L. to R: PCs 39 W.H. Pilliner, 28 H.N. Phillips, 45 G. Christopher, 42 J. A. Kelly, 44 T.H. Williams, 20 F.M. Bayley, 12 F.A. Jackson, 16 J.H. Stamp, 3 C.R. Moody, 31 J.R. Bayley, 72 T. Rees.

Front row, L. to R: PC 8 J. Bayliss, Sergeants 61 E.C. Wills, 40 J.E. Keyte, 6 A. Lewis, Inspector S.G. Whittaker, Superintendent and Deputy Chief Constable G.T. Brierley, Sergeants 32 A.T. Bullock, 48 J.J. White, PCs 7 T. Dix, 9 A.R. Smith

Above: PC 83 R. Weaver, served from 1938 to 1941. He was the youngest son of DCC A. Weaver.

Left: Gathering at Eastnor Castle for duty, on the occasion of the visit of Queen Mary to Herefordshire, on 26th. to 31st. July, 1937.
Back row, L. to R:
PCs 42 J.A. Kelly, 20 F.M. Bayley, 52 G.W.H. Hill, 43 G. W. Barker.
Seated: PC 5 J. Cole, Sergeant 32 A.T. Bullock

Below, Left: PC 76 R. Baugh, and companion.

Right:PCs 3 C.R. Moody, 67 F. Griffin, 45 G. Christopher, 57 J. Greenway.

WEOBLEY SECTION, ARMISTICE DAY PARADE, 1939.

Back row, L. to R: PC 39 R. Farmer, PC 13 W.J. Lines, FRPC 105 T. Probert .
Seated, L. to R: PC 19 A.C.J. Edwards, Sergeant 80 L.J. Jones, PC 71 A. F. Rock.
FRPC Probert, who had served in the Worcestershire Constabulary, became a First Reserve Constable in September 1939, continuing to serve until October 1943.

Below: PC 49 H.C. Bowery.

PC 4 J. H. Amos.
PC Amos was a former Welsh Guard, and a Heavy-weight boxer in the army. He was a POW in the second World War for several years, and, on his return, proved himself to be an able replacement for PC 1 C.F. Harris at Bishops Frome.
Picture taken outside the Five Bridges Inn, Much Cowarne.

Superintendent R. Strangward, with his wife Louisa, and seven of their eight children, about 1888.

Right:
Sergeant 23 W. Jones, with his wife Eliza, and daughter Martha, who was born in 1881. Photograph taken at Wigmore c.1885.

Below: Sergeant 46 J.H. Williams, reading to his daughter, Elizabeth May, in 1908.

Below: PC 23 J. Evans, with his son, in 1914, the year he left the Constabulary after eighteen years service. He joined the army and died as a result of wounds, in the early 1920's.

Above, Left: PC 39 L. James and family, c.1921. PC James joined the Constabulary in 1911, and was stationed at Steensbridge and Longtown in his early service. At the time of his retirement, in 1937, he was stationed at Kington.

Right: PC 57 J. Greenway, with his wife and children.

Below, Left: Sergeant 34 C.H. Matthews, with his wife and daughter.

Right: PC 92 J. Cook, with his wife and son, Brian.

Top, Left: PC 9 A.R. Smith, with his family, and Sergeant 73 H.D. Main.

Centre, Left: PC 79 G.A. Fletcher, with his son and daughter.

Above: PC 173 E.A. Hadley, at Burley Gate in 1962, with his daughter, Valerie, who was later to become the fourth generation of the family to join the police service. PC Hadley is the grand-son of PC 1 W.T. Hadley, and son of Inspector E.J. Hadley of Hereford City Police. A great-grand-son of W.T. Hadley served in the British South Africa Police, making a total of 120 years family police service.

Everyone off duty to attend the wedding of PC R. Farmer and former WAPC P. Brown, in 1946.

Back row: L. to R: T. Dix, F.J. Little, L.A. Workman, A.R. Smith.
Second row, L. to R: S.G. Whittaker, T.B. Wheeler, F. Griffin, F.A. Jackson, Miss I. Cole, Ms. E. Jones, Miss B. Hughes, Ms. G.M. Pratt, H.G. Venn, J.H. Amos, J.J. White, C.J. Andrews.

RURAL POLICE STATIONS.

Above: PC 12 W. Howard and family, outside Pembridge Police Station, about 1905.

Bredenbury Police Station, about 1925. Mrs. Hopkins, wife of PC 29 A. Hopkins, with her child.

Pontrilas Police Station in the 1930's. Evan Smith and his brother, the sons of PC 9 A.R. Smith

Below: Dilwyn Police Station, in the 1920's. Gwen Lewis, (Harding), daughter of PC 6 A. Lewis, with her companion.

Above: Bishops Frome Police Station
The last police occupant of this house was
PC 4 J.H. Amos.

Right: Cusop Police Station

Left: Burley Gate Police Station, pre-1940.

The Police Station was the right –hand side
of the pair of houses.

The last police officer to occupy this house
was PC 76 H.E.J. Penry.

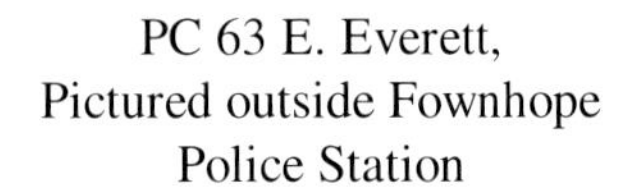

PC 63 E. Everett,
Pictured outside Fownhope
Police Station

WOMEN'S AUXILIARY POLICE CORPS.

WOMEN'S AUXILIARY POLICE CORPS.
HEADQUARTERS STAFF, ST. JOHN STREET, HEREFORD, JUNE 1942.
Back row, L. to R: WAPCs M. Brayshay, A.B. Dowse, M. Davies, M.T. Russell.
Front row, L. to R:WAPCs M. Cooper, F. White, P. Pitt.

Below, Left: WAPC B. Hughes Right: WAPCs E. Jones, K.M. Riley

WAR RESERVE CONSTABLES.

Above: WRPC 202 F.G. Irish.
Note the four war chevrons on his right sleeve. Served from 7-9-1939 until 31-12-1945, at Ross, then joined as a regular officer, PC101, in October 1947 until his early death in 1949.
Right: WRPC 210 E.J. Hawker. War Reserve Constable at Ross, 1939-1945. A former water-bailiff he had served in the army in the 1914-1918 War, and was known as a keen marks-man.

Below, Right: WRPC 228 F. Mills. After a short spell at Kington he assisted with the Lyonshall beat for two years until 1944, when he moved to Eardisley and worked that beat, alone, until 1946.
Below, Left: WRPC 230 R.W. Tanner, was a former Special Constable, who worked on the Mobile Section from November 1941, until called into the army in 1944.

Above, L: WRPC 214 R.H. Spencer, who transferred from the Metropolitan Police in August 1942, worked the Callow beat before moving to Weston-under-Penyard.
Above,R: R.W. Page of Leominster, pictured as a Special Inspector after the war. He had pre-war service as a Special Constable and was a War Reserve Constable, at Leominster from 1941 to 1943. He later became Commandant of the Special Constabulary at Leominster

Below, Right: WRPC 223 T.F. Littlar, was based at Leominster from March 1942 to March 1946.
Below, Left: WRPC 231 G.R. Bennett, served at Ross from 1941 to 1945.

SPECIAL CONSTABULARY.

ABBEYDORE SECTION OF THE SPECIAL CONSTABULARY, c.1945.
Brigadier General T.R.F. Bate, CMG, Commandant of the Special Constabulary throughout the war, in the centre of the front row, flanked by the Chief Constable and Deputy Chief Constable.
(Photograph by G.W. Alderson, Hereford).

Below, Top picture: Ledbury Section, 1944. Bottom picture: Weobley section, c.1944.

A representative contingent of all sections of the Special Constabulary marching-past the saluting dais in High Town, Hereford, on the occasion of parade celebrating the Centenary of the formation of the Herefordshire Constabulary, Sunday, April 7th. 1957.

Below,L: Special Commandant Major K.G. Stacey Hatfield, of Ledbury, 1957. R: Special Inspector A.J.T. Richards, of Leominster, served as a War Reserve Constable at Ledbury from 1940 to 1945.

POLICE WOMEN

(Photograph reproduced by courtesy of The Hereford Times).

The first Police-Women to be appointed, 1947.
Back row, L. to R: PW 6 R.E. Smith, PW 8 E.M. Watkins, PW 11 E.S. Phillips, PW 7 O.M. Hughes, PW 9 W.A. Garrett, PW 10 P. Jones-Newton.
Front row, L. to R: PW 4 M.T. Oxton, WDC 3 J. Edwards, DCC T.B. Wheeler, Chief Constable F. Newton, PWSergeant 1 D.B. Simpson, PW 2 K. Elias, PW 5 D. Slater.

PW Sergeant 1 D.B. Simpson.

PW 7 O.M. Hughes.

PW 8 E.M. Watkins.

PW 11 E.S. Phillips

Left: PW 2 M.A. Morris, served from 1965-1966

Right: PW 9 M.C. Nelson,
became the wife of PC 214 T.S. Moses

Below: PW 8 B. Wheatley,
on traffic control at Ross.

Above, Left: PS 61 E.C. Wills, instructing school children in cycling proficiency.
Above, Right: Sergeant 17 C. Foster, transferred from Doncaster Borough Police in 1939, was promoted Chief Inspector in 1951 and Superintendent in 1958.

Below: Sergeants 30 E.E. Bendall and 45 G. Christopher, pictured at Leominster. They were two of the original four on the new mobile section in 1931.

Right: Sergeant 31 J.R. Bayley, joined the Constabulary in October 1931. He is pictured outside Ledbury Police Station (*on the left*), about 1942.

MOBILE SECTION.

Right: PC 65 G. Williams, who was based at Leominster, astride one of the first Sunbeam motor-cycles to be used for patrol duties, about 1931. It is understandable that he earned the nickname 'Speedy'.

Below: PC 65 G. Williams, photographed outside Wigmore Police Station, about 1935, with a Morris 10 hp car, used in the Leominster Division.

Bottom of page: These four cars, two Morris 10 hp and two Rover 14 hp, were purchased from County Motors, Hereford, in 1937. Left to Right: PC 55 D.H. Roberts, PC 65 G. Williams, PC 47 W. Franzen, PC 18 F.G. Stephens, Inspector T.B. Wheeler.

Top, L. to R: PC 67 F. J. Griffin,
PC 18 F.G. Stephens,
PC 55 D.H. Roberts.

Right, L. to R:
PC 12 F.A. Jackson,
PC 39 R. Farmer,
PC 21 J.S. Bourne
with a Pontiac car purchased during the war, and kept for a short time afterwards

Below: PC 12 F. A. Jackson, with Austin Divisional car.

TRAFFIC DEPARTMENT.

Left, L. to R:
PC 7 R.V. Beekar,
PC 113 G.J. Wood,
with Austin patrol car about 1950.`

Lower Left, L. to R:
PCs 80 T. Batho,
113 G.J. Wood,
129 L.H. Taylor,
Sgt. 119 C. H. Hoskins.
Cyril Hoskins joined the Birmingham City Police in 1921. He came to Hereford City Police in 1924 and was the first motor-cycle patrolman in the City. He had also been a police-fireman and drove one of the fire-engines. In 1947, after the merger, he became a Sergeant on the Traffic Department, where he stayed until he completed his regular police service in 1960. He continued as a First Police Reserve, until 1972 – a total of 51 years police service.

Below, L. to R:
Ps 119 C. H. Hoskins,
PC 109 M.J. Read

Right:
Sergeant 109 M.J. Read,
with Austin
Patrol car.
M.J. Read joined Hereford City Police in 1946, after leaving the RAF. He became part of the Herefordshire Constabulary in 1947, and after service as a beat officer, was promoted Sergeant on the Traffic Department in 1958.
He retired in 1976.

L. to R:
PC 18 K.J. Hursey,
PC 36 D. Massam.

Ken Hursey joined the Constabulary in 1949, and retired in 1979. After serving as a beat officer in the City, he spent several years on the Traffic Department. He then became a Detective Constable on 'Scenes of Crime' Dept. He is an all-round sportsman, well remembered for his football skills.

INSPECTION OF TRAFFIC DEPARTMENT, AT HEADQUARTERS.

L. to R: PS 116 A.B. Roberts, PS 21 J.S. Bourne, PC 146 D.W. Evans, PC 75 H. Bufton, PC 32 E.H.J. Clinton, PC 20 J.F. Pritchard, PC 122 C.A. White, PC 10 B.S. Williams, PC 25 T.R. Mash, PC 190 B.W. Thomas, PC 177 D.G. Banks, PC 134 C. V. Lloyd, PC 185 A. Drew ?, P.C 17 J.P.C. Dolan, PC 18 K. Hursey, PC 7 W. Gurney.

PC 117 A.G.W. Matthews and PC 10 B. S. Williams at work in the Control–room at Headquarters, about 1955. The control-room was manned throughout the 24 hours, and was the hub of Constabulary communications, keeping in radio contact with all the patrol cars. The information contained there was the envy of other Forces, who made frequent use of the resources, when requiring help.

CENTENARY MARCH-PAST, 7th. APRIL 1957.
Traffic Department and Headquarters Department, led by Chief-Inspector C. Foster and Inspector F.J. Griffin, salute the Lord Lieutenant of Herefordshire, Sir Richard Cotterell, Bart., in High Town, Hereford, following the service in the Cathedral.

INSPECTION OF TRAFFIC DEPARTMENT BY HER MAJESTY'S INSPECTOR, 1966.

L. to R:
PC 180 M.R. Wood,
PC 3 R. Taylor,
PC 120 S.E. Baggett,
A/Sgt. 106 C.G. Davies,
HMI, Mr. N. Galbraith,
CC R. McCartney,
PS 136 B. Gradwell,
Supt. C.W. Wallin.

L. to R: Sergeant 44 G.R. Gough, PC 52 C.H.W. Maddy, PC 77 R.J.T. Jones, PC 105 D.H. Thomas, PC 84 W. Deakin, PC 194 P.B.P. Holman, PC 171 C.B. Wood, PC 167 F.R. Powell, PC 134 C.V. Lloyd, PC 180 M.R. Wood, PC 3 R. Taylor, PC 120 S.E. Baggett.

L. to R., facing camera: PC 77 R.J.T. Jones, PC 105 D.H. Thomas, PC 84 W. Deakin, PC 194 P.B.P. Holman, PC 171 C.B. Wood, PC 167 F.R. Powell, 134 C.V. Lloyd.

Above, Left: PC 38 E. Cobbe, a native of Dublin, who joined the Constabulary in 1946, after service in the Parachute Regiment. He became a Chief Inspector, and retired at Shrewsbury.
Above, Right: Superintendent E.D.H. Walters, was Superintendent at Leominster from 1941 until his death in 1951, aged 54 years.
Below, Left: PC 85 A.H.Cousins, joined the County Constabulary in 1947, after the merger with the Hereford City Police, and was the first County-appointed Constable to be posted into the city. He is pictured wearing a County tunic and a City helmet.
Right: PC 55 D.H. Roberts. Prior to WW2 PC Roberts was part of the Mobile Section. After his release from the army he was posted to Bosbury, and in 1947 was promoted to Detective Sergeant. At the time of his retirement in 1965 he was Chief Inspector in charge of the Traffic Department.

KINGTON SECTION, about 1946.
Back row, L. to R: PC 40 D.W. Harvey, PC 92 J. Cook, PC 9 G. Janes.
Front row, L. to R: PC 29 A. Hopkins, Sergeant 34 D. Grigg, PC 54 W.J. Evans.

Below, Left: PC 92 J. Cook, Sergeant 23 H. Arrowsmith, WRPC 233 C.B. Pearce.

Below, Right: Inspector C.W. Wallin. C.W. Wallin, a native of Herefordshire, joined the West Riding Constabulary in 1930. He transferred to the Herefordshire Constabulary in 1939, as Sergeant/Clerk at Leominster. In 1942 he was promoted to Inspector at Headquarters, and in 1958 became Superintendent at Ross. In 1960 he became Deputy Chief Constable, staying on after the merger in 1967, to become Chief Superintendent, in charge of Hereford 'E' Division, West Mercia Constabulary.

Officers of Central Division parading for His Majesty's Inspector, Mr. F.T. Tarry, in the Drill-yard behind Hereford Police Station, in 1951.

Recipients of the new Long Service and Good Conduct Awards, at Ledbury, January 1953.

Back row, L. to R: PC 62 D. Evans, PC 71 A.F. Rock, PC 77 H.J. James.
Seated, L. to R: Former PC 3 C.R. Moody, Inspector E.C. Wills, Sergeant 12 F.A. Jackson.

Retirement of Superintendent F. Wheatley, 1952.
L. to R: Chief Constable F. Newton, Supt. F. Wheatley, Deputy Chief Constable T.B. Wheeler, Supt. K.C. Weaver.

Supt. Wheatley joined the Hove Borough Police in 1919, and transferred to Hereford City Police, in 1921, to become Sergeant/Chief Clerk. On the amalgamation of the City and County Forces, in 1947, he became Superintendent in charge of Central Division. He was succeeded by Superintendent K.C. Weaver.

PC 8 A.J. Williams.
Taken prisoner-of-war for four and a half years while serving with the Welsh Guards in WW2, he was afterwards awarded the BEM. He joined Herefordshire Constabulary in 1946.

Right: L. ro R: PC 24 M.A. Barter and PC 75 H. Bufton.

PC Barter joined Herefordshire Constabulary in 1924. At the time of his retirement in 1952 he was stationed at Allensmore.

PC Bufton began his police career in the Metropolitan Police in 1935, before transferring to Herefordshire in 1939. He retired in 1966.

PC 48 M.T. Ovens, *(left),* who joined the Constabulary in 1950, and his brother, PC 100 N.G. Ovens, were the fourth generation of the Ovens family to join the police service. After retirement, in 1975, Michael Ovens continued as a civilian in the Administrative Support Unit. PC 100 N.G. Ovens began his police service in Herefordshire Constabulary in 1960, and served in several departments in Herefordshire, including becoming the first Crime Prevention Officer. Prior to the merger in 1967 he was promoted Inspector, and took charge of the control-room at Hindlip, before becoming Detective Chief Inspector at the Regional Crime Intelligence Office, in Birmingham. His next move was to take charge of Shrewsbury and Telford Divisions, as Superintendent, before moving to the Traffic Department as Chief Superintendent. Later he headed the Operational Support Unit, followed by CID. In 1980 Mr. Ovens became Assistant Chief Constable of Staffordshire Constabulary, and in May 1984 he was appointed Deputy Chief Constable of Cheshire Constabulary. He took up his last post, as Chief Constable of Lincolnshire, in July 1990, retiring in 1993. His daughter served in West Mercia, and his son is a serving officer in Staffordshire.

The contingent of police from Herefordshire Constabulary on the way to London for duty on Coronation Day, 2nd. June, 1953.

Front row, L. to R: Inspector H.J. Harris, BEM, Sergeant 25 W.R. Wakefield, PC 38 E. Cobbe, PC 17 J.P.C. Dolan, PC 79 G.A. Fletcher, PC 32 E.H.J. Clinton, PC 2 L.T. Whitworth, PC 118 G.W.F. Thomas, PC 4 J.H. Amos, PC 117 A.G.W. Matthews, PC 154 A.W. Sherred, PW 4. M. Oxton.
Others who travelled, but are not clearly shown on the photograph were:
Sergeant 111 T.H. Stevens, PC 42 J.A. Kelly, PC 140 D.W. Strang, PC 16 J.H. Stamp, PC 15 H.J. Scrine, PC 74 D.F. Eastlake, PC 88 C.E. Dominey, PC 160 B.E. Salisbury, PC 23 G.D. Surrell, PC 19 H.J. Cole.

(This photograph is reproduced by courtesy of The Hereford Times).

Left: PC 152 J.F.G. Barnett, outside Bishop's Frome Police Station, during the hop-picking season, 1953.
PC Barnett later served with the CID, becoming Detective Sergeant. In 1965 he was promoted uniformed Inspector at Leominster, and afterwards became Chief Superintendent in West Mercia Constabulary.

Right: DC 170 J. Bayford
And PC 35 J.R.I. Clinton

SENIOR CONSTABLE'S COURSE, AT HEADQUARTERS, 1952.
Back row, L. to R: PC 113 G. J. Wood, PC 88 C. E. Dominey, PC 53 L. Powell, PC 87 W.J. Williams, PC 115 A. Deakin.
Middle row, L. to R: PC 37 A.E. Matthews, PC 79 G. Fletcher, PC 26 C.J. Andrews, PC 117 A.G.W. Matthews, PC 16 J.H. Stamp, PC 139 P. Bristow.
Seated, L. to R: Insp. F.M. Bayley, Insp. D.A. Pickard, DCC T.B. Wheeler, CC F. Newton, C/Insp. C. Foster, Insp. F.J. Griffin, Sgt. 131 T.S. Davies.

SENIOR CONSTABLE'S COURSE, AT HEADQUARTERS, 1953.
Back row, L. to R: PC 112 V.K. Pearce, PC 126 R.J. Garrett, PC 15 H.J. Scrine, PC 86 H.G. Venn, PC 39 R. Farmer.
Middle row, L. to R: PC 140 D. Strang, PC 116 A.B. Roberts, PC 120 J. Trumper, PC 4 J.H. Amos, PC 43 G.W. Barker, PC 62 D. Evans, PC 92 J. Cook.
Front row, L. to R: Sgt. 131 T.S. Davies, Det.Insp. R.J. Weaver, DCC T.B. Wheeler, CC F. Newton, Ch.Insp. C. Foster, Insp. F.J. Griffin, Sgt. 81 D.A. Gibson.

Recipients of the new Long Service and Good Conduct Award, at Hereford, 1953.
Back row, L. to R: Former Sergeant 103 E.J. Cousins, Sergeant 119 C.H. Hoskins, PC 112 V.K. Pearce, PC 115 A. Deakin, PC 136 A. Glazzard, PC 123 P. Jenkins, PC 127 R. Bowler, Sergeant 130 A.V. Lucas, Sergeant 106 B. James.
Seated, L. to R: Inspector F.J. Griffin, Former Superintendent F. Wheatley, Chief Constable F. Newton, The Right Worshipful the Mayor of Hereford, Mr. A.E. Farr, Deputy Chief Constable T.B. Wheeler, Det.Inspector R.J. Weaver, Inspector H.J. Harris, Inspector G. Christopher.
(This photograph reproduced courtesy of The Hereford Times).

Left: Inspector F.J. Griffin joined the Constabulary in 1929, and was stationed at Whitchurch and Leominster before joining the staff of the Hereford Divisional Headquarters. He was one of the first four officers selected for the Mobile Section in 1931, and when the Traffic Department was formed in 1947 he took control and stayed with the department until his retirement in 1959, taking an active interest in Road Safety and Cycle Proficiency training.
Right: PC 97 G.A. Birch and PC 82 H. Broadhead, leaving Ashperton Police Station, on cycle patrol.

Photograph reproduced by courtesy of Geoffrey Hammonds, Hereford.

SOUTHERN DIVISION, 1953.

Back row, L. to R: PCs 97 G.A. Birch, 153 G.J. Nash, 89 K.F. Brooks, 11 R. N. Lane, 172 W.J. Osborn, 57 P.J. Noakes, 59 S.G. Perks, 178 J.A.M. Main, 78 J.C. Vernalls.

Second row, L. to R: PCs 91 K.W. Campbell, 166 P. Batterbee, 46 K.W. Leak, 155 W.J. Hillstead, 99 G.F. Middleton, 149 G.N. Murrie, 49 J.H. Down, 65 A.J. Winnel, 48 M.T. Ovens, 151 J.J. Preece, 51 C.C. Boughton.

Third row, Left, L. to R: PCs 164 D.A.L. Johnson, 17 J.P.C. Dolan, 38 E. Cobbe, 101 R. Colwell, 34 G. Sanders. Right, L. to R: PCs 88 C.E. Dominey, 32 E.H.J. Clinton, 159 J.C.C. Cole, 100 S.C. Mace, 175 N. Shutt.

Seated, L. to R: DC 90 A.L. Drennen, DS 132 R.G. Kendle, PC 62 D. Evans, Sgt. 82 H. Broadhead, PS 1 G. Nunn, PS 14 A. Moss, Insp. E.C. Wills, DCC T.B. Wheeler, Chief Constable F. Newton, Supt. A. Lewis, Insp. D. Grigg, PS 28 H.N. Phillips, PS 76 H.E.J. Penry, DC 47 G. Painter, PW 12 G.E. McDougall, PW 9 B.V. Mash.

Above:
PC 173 E.A. Hadley
and
PC 67 S. Roberts.

Pictured with the
Nelson family during the
hop-picking season at
Bishops Frome, in 1954.

In 1958 PC Roberts volunteered
for twenty-one months temporary
service with the
Cyprus Police.

PC 83 A.W.C. Morris
at Bromyard Police
Station, 1951.

Above, Right: A convivial moment at Brampton Brian Point-to-Point Races, 1955.
L. to R: PC 22 J.A. Bull, PC 4 J.H. Amos, PC 16 J.H. Stamp, PC 26 C.J. Andrews, PC 9 G. Janes,
PC 50 G. Lawrence, PC 43 G.W. Barker, PC 87 W.J. Williams, PS 58 A. Mangham.

L. to R:
PC 110 G.B. Todd,
PC 20 J. Pritchard,
Sergeant 111 T.H. Stevens,
PC 137 D. Young,

Sergeant Stevens joined the
Hereford City Police in 1932, and
after the amalgamation continued
his service in the Herefordshire
Constabulary until 1962.
For many years he was a
prominent member of police
football and cricket teams.

Ross-on-Wye, c.1952.
L. to R: PC 67 D.J. Irish,
WPC 12 G.E. McDougall,
PC 152 J.F.G. Barnett,
PC 164 D.A.L. Johnson.
PC Irish was the son of the late PC 101 F.G. Irish, of Ross. Shortly after this photograph was taken he joined the Kenya Police.

Below, Left: HM Queen Elizabeth the Second leaving the Dean Leigh Canteen, in Hereford, during her visit to the county in 1957.
CC F. Newton on the right.

PC 10 B.S. Williams, at Bromyard.

PC 173 E.A. Hadley, WPC 10 M.A. Rowlands and PC 15 H.J. Scrine, Outside Leominster Police Station, c.1956.
R: PC 39 R. Farmer. In 1952, investigating a disturbance at Bromyard, he received a shot-gun wound to the thigh. He later made a full recovery.

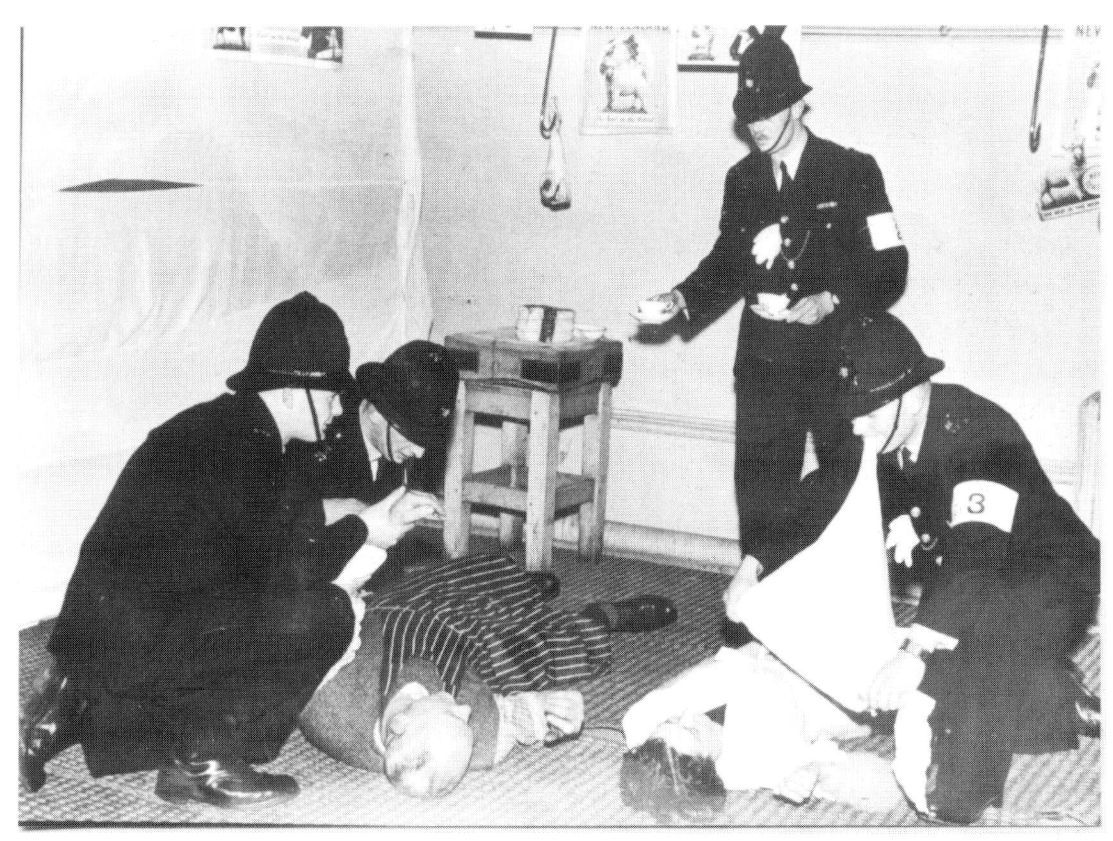

Competition in First Aid, for the Devereux Trophy, Shire Hall Hereford, 1953.
The theme of the supposed incident was that a butcher, (PC 95 Sid. Humphries), had collapsed in his shop after having cut himself badly. A lady customer (WPC 7 Olive M. Hughes) walked into the shop, and on seeing the blood, promptly fainted, striking her head on the way down. PC 167 Claud Morgan, (bending over the butcher), was assisted by PC 171 J. Maynard, PC 133 Glyn Morris tended the lady patient, and PC 122 Colin A. White brought in the tea.
(Photograph reproduced courtesy of A. Royden Willetts, ARPS)

L. to R:
Chief Inspector D.A. Gibson, Detective Inspector N. Davies and Sergeant 138 A.G. Roberts, examine some of the weapons handed in during a fire-arms amnesty, in August 1961.

Sergeant 30 E.E. Bendall, completed his service at Bromyard in 1957.

Who says 'A Policeman's Lot is not a Happy One'?

L. to R: PCs 136 B. Gradwell, 179 D.G. Groves, 103 P. Devenish, 178 J.A.M. Main, 76 G.T. Warley, 160 F. Davies.

Left: PC 120 J. Trumper, joined the Hereford City Police in 1937, and became HM Coroners Officer. After war service he resumed his duties with the Coroner, continuing them in the County Constabulary after the 1947 merger until his retirement in 1962.
Right: PC 160 F. Davies, joined the Constabulary in 1955, after army service, and took over the duties of Coroner's Officer after PC Trumper.

Both these men were well respected for their compassion and for the help which they gave to bereaved families.

The new Police Station at Ross-on-Wye, built at a cost of £25,413, which was opened in 1957.

Pictured below are the police officers and dignitaries who attended the occasion.

Back row, L. to R: Inspector D. Grigg, Mr. H. Vaughan, (*Builder*), Mr. W. Usher, *(County Architect)*, Mr. R.C. Hansen, *(Clerk of the Peace)*, Mr. F.T. Tarry, *HMI*, Preb. G.S. Stockley, *(Rector of Ross)*, Superintendent A. Lewis.
Seated: Chief Constable, F. Newton, Mr. W.H. Cornish, *(Home Office)*, Lord Cilcennin, *(Lord Lieutenant of Herefordshire)*, Alderman D.W. Hamlen Williams, *(Chairman of the County Council)*.

The parade held to mark the Centenary of Herefordshire Constabulary,
High Town, Hereford, 7th. April, 1957.
The salute was taken by Sir Richard Cotterell, Bart., Lord Lieutenant of Herefordshire, accompanied by the Right Worshipful the Mayor of Hereford, Councillor C.J. Gooding,
and the Worshipful the Mayor of Leominster, Councillor D.R. Jones.

Below: Members of Northern Division, led by Superintendent J.E. Keyte and Inspector F.J. Little, march past the saluting dais.

(Photograph reproduced by courtesy of The Hereford Times.)

Members of Central Division , led by Superintendent K.C. Weaver and Inspector C.W. Wallin, march past the saluting dais.

Below: Members of Southern Division, led by Superintendent A. Lewis and Inspector E. Wills, march past the saluting dais.

1957

HEREFORDSHIRE CONSTABULARY – CENTENARY 1957

Back row L. to R.- P.C.'s 147 Reid, 186 Osborne, 96 Smith, 15 Scrine, 139 Bristow, 24 Watkins, 22 Bull, 37 Matthews, 140 Strang, 118 Mauvan, 74 Eastlake, 128 Neal, 19 Cole, *C. of A.*, 121 Tasker, 42 Clements, 98 Gobourn, 59 Perks, 60 Baylis, 184 Daniels, 92 Cook, 43 Barker, 34 Sanders, 175 Shutt, 182 Joseph, 68 Andrews

Second row L. to R. – PCs 126 Garrett, 168 Walsh, 187 Evans, 169 Wallace, 87 Williams, 180 Wood, 193 Craig, 69 Jones, 127 Thwaites, 27 Everett, 54 Rees, 166 Diffey, 25 Mash, 110 Todd, *C. of A.*, 50 Lawrence, 106 Davies, 172 Osborn, 171 Wood, 9 Janes, 61 Baker, 159 Cole, 57 Noakes, 66 Winney, 20 Pritchard, 78 Vernalls, 85 Cousins

Third row L. to R.– PCs 95 Humphries, 44 Gough, 13 Williams, 136 Gradwell, 185 Drew, 71 Button, 76 Warley, 112 Pearce, 179 Groves, 105 Thomas, 2 Whitworth, 103 Devenish, 107 Tipton, 73 Densham, 153 Nash, 125 Carter, 143 Stainer, 190 Thomas, 62 Evans, 51 Boughton 160 Davies, 173 Hadley, 8 Williams,16 Stamp, 11 Lane, 89 Brooks, 38 Cobbe, 88 Dominey, 189 Davies, Cadet Watts

Fourth row L. to R.– Cadets Jones, Edwards, PCs 188 Woodman, 174 Deakin, 178 Main, 183 Derry, 162 Joyce, 63 Short, 176 Paton, 137 Young, 181 Herbert, 145 Morrisey, 67 Roberts, 53 Burley, 4 Amos, 26 Andrews, 40 Jordan, 79 Fletcher, 6 Cook, 86 Venn, 77 James, 35 Clinton, 45 Cain, 99 Middleton, 192 Parker, 194 Holman. 151 Preece, 155 Hillstead, 123 Jenkins, 94 Mercer, Cadet Wright

Fifth row L. to R.– PCs 18 Hursey, 167 Morgan, 10 Williams, 129 Taylor, 36 Massam, 133 Morris, 32 Clinton, 7 Gurney, 64 Bowdley, 177 Banks, 83 Morris, 109 Read, 48 Ovens, 191 Talbot, 161 Hall, 65 Winnel, 157 Whent, 49 Down, 154 Sherred, 117 Matthews, 150 Burgess, 144 Norris, 46 Hepworth, 21 Bourne, 122 White, 29 Kedward, 17 Dolan, 158 Pikes, 135 Harding, 146 Evans, 93 Arrowsmith, 80 Batho

Sixth row L. to R.– WPCs 4 Oxton, 11 Phillips, 8 Wheatley, 12 McDougall, P.Sgts. 75 Bufton, 81 Gibson, 116 Roberts, 131 Davies, 70 Holman, 14 Moss, 115 Deakin, 102 Eley, 111 Stevens, 12 Jackson, 72 Rees, 1 Nunn, 31 Bayley, 52 Hill, 114 Whittall, 90 Drennen, 138 Roberts, 58 Mangham, 130 Lucas, 56 Workman, 39 Farmer, 82 Broadhead, 23 Surrell, 119 Hoskins, WPCs 2 Fishpool, 7 Hughes, 5 Slater, 10 Rowlands

Front row L.to R.– Cadet Broadhead, WPSgt. 3 Edwards, DCs 156 Keyte, 47 Painter, 152 Barnett, 142 Benbow, DSgt. 124 Davies, D.I. Weaver, Insps. Bayley, Christopher, Wills, C.I. Foster, Supt. Weaver, D.C.C. Wheeler, C.C. Freeman Newton, Supts. Lewis, Keyte, Insps. Grigg, Wallin,Griffin, Little, PSgt. 5 Cole, D.Sgts. 132 Kendle, 55 Roberts, 84 Lappage, DCs 141 Lawley, 108 Jones, 170 Bayford

(Photographed at the Parade Ground, Fire Station, St. Owen St., Hereford)

Chief Constable F. Newton and Deputy Chief Constable T.B. Wheeler,
on the occasion of the Centenary Celebrations.
T.B. Wheeler joined the Herefordshire Constabulary on Armistice Day, 1918, and during his forty years of police service rose from Constable to Deputy Chief Constable. He maintained a keen interest in the police football and cricket teams, and was well-known in Hereford bowling circles.

Below, The new Chief Constable, Robert McCartney, with his deputy, Superintendent K.C. Weaver, pictured with the retiring Chief Constable, Mr. Freeman Newton. Superintendent and Deputy Chief Constable K.C. Weaver was the son of the late Superintendent and Deputy Chief Constable A. Weaver, and the younger brother of Chief Inspector R.J. Weaver, of Hereford City Police. Supt. Weaver started his police career in 1928 as a civilian clerk, and the following year was appointed PC17, becoming a clerk at Headquarters. He served at Leominster from 1930 to 1935, and after his return to Hereford he became a Sergeant in 1937, and Inspector in 1939. From 1942 to 1945 he served in RAF Bomber Command. In 1951 he became Superintendent in charge of the Northern (Leominster) Division, returning to Hereford in 1952 to take charge of the Central (Hereford) Division. He became the Deputy Chief Constable on the retirement of Superintendent Wheeler.

(Photograph reproduced by courtesy of The Hereford Times).

Left: PC 107 T.R. Tipton preparing for point-duty at the Iron Cross, Leominster.

Right: PC 132 A.J.F. Buttriss on point-duty at the Red Lion junction in Hereford.

Below, right: PC 118 D.W. Mauvan, at the Red Lion junction, Hereford.
The traffic lights at this junction were, for many years, the only ones in the whole of the county of Herefordshire.

Below, Left: Inspector D. Grigg overseeing Cycle Proficiency Training at Ross.

VISIT OF HER MAJESTY'S INSPECTOR, ROSS-ON-WYE, 13th MAY, 1959.

General Inspection by Senior Officers,

L. to R:
Superintendent C.W. Wallin,

Chief Constable R. McCartney,

Inspector D.Grigg,

Her Majesty's Inspector,
F.T. Tarry, CBE.

Officers facing HMI,
F.T. Tarry, CBE.

L. to R:

Sergeant 52 G.W.H. Hill,

Sergeant 59 S.G. Perks,

PC 65 A.J. Winnel,

PC 125 D.C.S. Carter,

PC 145 L.F. Morrisey

Facing camera,
L. to R:

Chief Constable R. McCartney,

Superintendent C.W. Wallin,

Her Majesty's Inspector,
F.T. Tarry, CBE.

Inspector D. Grigg.

All photographs on this page appear by courtesy of G.L. WARD.

Above, Left: Sergeant 141 K. Lawley, joined the Hereford City Police in 1941, and after war service in the Fleet Air Arm attaining the rank of Petty Officer, returned to Hereford. Following the 1947 amalgamation he was transferred to Central Division CID, and became well-known for his twenty months investigation into the 'RAF Bread Scandal', for which he was commended by Mr. Justice Stable.
Above, Right: Detective Sergeant 132 R.G. Kendle, a former Coldstream Guard, joined Hereford City Police in 1935, and was recalled to the army during WW2, reaching the rank of Captain. After the amalgamation he became Detective Sergeant at Ross, then Inspector in the Southern Division, and finally Chief Inspector at Hereford, until his retirement in 1966.

Below, Left and Right Sergeant 52 G.W.H. Hill and Sergeant 47 G. Painter, at Ross Police Station.

The first
Beat Officers Motor-cycle Course,
at Bridgend, Glamorgan, in 1960.

L. to R:
PC 180 M.R. Wood,
PC 44 G.R. Gough,
PC 184 F.G. Daniels,
PC 49 J.H. Down,
PC 113 G.J. Wood,
PC 34 G. Sanders.

Left: PC 49 J.H. Down,
on a Velocette motor-cycle outside Harewood
End Police Station.

Below: PC 85 A.H. Cousins, the Fownhope
beat officer, pictured in Hafod Road, Hereford,
with a radio-equipped DMW motor-cycle,
specially manufactured to police requirements.

Above, Left: PC 44 G.R. Gough, with DMW motor-cycle, pictured outside Upton Bishop Police Station,
one of the first post-WW2 rural stations to be built.

Inspector G.H. Holman,
Inspector C.H. Lappage
and
Inspector J. Cole,
leading the parade to the
TA Centre, Harold Street,
Hereford,
for Inspection by
HMI F.T. Tarry, CBE.,
February 1962.

(Photograph reproduced by courtesy of The Hereford Times).

Left:
PC 57 P.J. Noakes
in 1959,
leaving Bredwardine
Police Station
for cycle patrol.

Awaiting the arrival of the Mayor,
outside Hereford Town Hall.
Inspector G. Painter
and PC 131 B.S. Humphreys.

Above: Chief Inspector D.A. Gibson, at his desk. A native of Northern Ireland, he served in the Irish Guards before joining the Herefordshire Constabulary in 1936. During his war-time service in the Irish Rifles, he was promoted to Major, before receiving severe wounds which necessitated a prolonged stay in hospital.

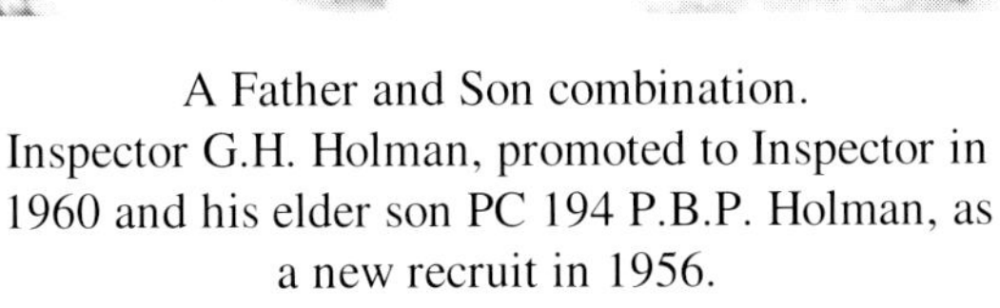

A Father and Son combination.
Inspector G.H. Holman, promoted to Inspector in 1960 and his elder son PC 194 P.B.P. Holman, as a new recruit in 1956.

Between 1965 and 1968 a Regional Mobile Column was in existence, for Civil Defence purposes. Annual training took place, in the Midlands, and the unit was completely self- contained, being made up of police officers who had previous experience as tradesmen, cooks, signallers, drivers, first-aiders etc.
The aim of the column was primarily for Civil Defence, but it could assist at any major civil incident.
At the time of the Aberfan disaster, in October 1966, five members of Herefordshire Constabulary were with the unit at its annual training camp, when the unit was immediately diverted to South Wales to render assistance. Members of the column remained in the area, for nine days, until after the visit of HM the Queen to Aberfan.

Top:
Sergeant 145 L.F. Morrisey and
PC 81 E. Owen.

Centre, Left:PC 105 D.H. Thomas

Centre, Right:
PC 194 P.B.P. Holman
(on the right).

Right:
PC 162 C. Joyce, in charge of
catering arrangements.

Left to Right: Inspector J. Cole, Chief Inspector F.M. Bayley, Superintendent C. Foster.

Inspector E.Wills.

Superintendent J.E. Keyte.

Superintendent T. Rees.

Chief Inspector J. Keyte, the nephew of J.E. Keyte, joined the Herefordshire Constabulary in 1948, after service as a Police Cadet, and National Service. Following early years in uniform, he transferred to CID, then on to the Training Department and Administration, and was Chief Inspector at the time of the amalgamation in 1967. He became Deputy Commander of Telford Division in West Mercia Constabulary, and later was in charge of the Worcester Division. Mr. Keyte was a Police Federation representative in each rank, taking the Chair of the Joint Board for eight years, and becoming involved with the work of the Superintendents Association, when he was promoted to the rank, in 1968. Subsequently he has been adviser on police matters to several Home Secretaries, has presented evidence to Royal Commissions, and was the first Chairman of the Police Negotiation Board. For eight years, prior to his retirement in 1985, he was national secretary of the Superintendents Association.
For his services to the police he was awarded the OBE in 1984.

PC 178 J.A.M. Main, with one of the first Panda cars in the City of Hereford.
Although the neighbourhood beat system was planned well beforehand it had barely started at the time of the 1967 amalgamation.

TRAFFIC WARDENS.
Back row, L. to R: H. Lawrence, D. Begg, E. Green, M. Hart, W.M. Mason, B. Sanders, J. Rowley, PC J.S.M. Morris.
Seated, L. to R: A. Wheatstone, M. Jones, Sergeant W.M. Cain, J. Bishop, M. Williams, R.F. Griffin.

This photograph was taken in the early 1970's but is included because most of the original ten Traffic Wardens are shown.

PC 42 D.T. Allen with Major, and PC 36 G.T. Lewis with Simba, photographed in the grounds of 'Brockington', Police Headquarters, Hereford, shortly after completing their training.

SPORT and LEISURE.

In the early years of the Constabulary conditions of service, and lack of transport facilities precluded participation in organised police sporting activities, but gradually such activities were encouraged and became a popular part of leisure time. Football originally took precedence, and several members of the police team have been of the standard to gain a trial with professional clubs or have played some games for Hereford United. Mr. Freeman Newton had been instrumental in providing cricket equipment early in the 1930s, and from then on the game had a regular place in the sporting fixtures, along with other games and sports and pastimes such as rugby, snooker, darts and crib, bowls, shooting, swimming, golf, badminton, angling, athletics, tennis, table tennis, bell-ringing and photography.

Individual sports have also had an important place. Charlie Morris, who had been an Army Cadet Champion boxer in his youth, competed in the British Open Police Boxing Championships, at the Empire Pool, Wembley, in 1951, as a light heavy-weight, and was unfortunate to be beaten in the semi-final by the Irish ABA Champion, O'Riordan.
Norman Shutt, who was captain of the police athletics team, was given special leave in 1955 when he was one of thirty selected to train for the British Winter Olympics ski-ing team, and was chosen to represent Great Britain at the Cortina Olympics in 1956. In the early 1960's Archie Buttriss became prominent in the sports of Shot-putt and Discus throwing. In 1963 he was Police and Welsh National Champion in both events, breaking previous records. He repeated the double performance the following year, but did not break his record.

The Social Fund was set up in April 1947 'to provide for the mental and physical recreation of members of the Fund, and to supply testimonials to retiring members of ten shillings for each completed years service, to a maximum of fifteen pounds'. It was the intention to also consider the grant of testimonials to persons who came to the assistance of the police. The membership fee was set at one shilling per week, and amounts were decided upon to cover transport and meals for sporting events.

Families looked forward to the Annual Sports Day held at the Police Sports Ground in Hereford, when grown-ups and children could enjoy the various games and sports provided for their entertainment, and the high-light of the social year for many children was the Christmas party organised in each Division by the Welfare Committee, when every child received a present from Father Christmas.

The Newton Police Garden Cup was presented for the first time in 1952, and annually thereafter, and keen gardeners endeavoured to have their garden looking at its best when the judges came round, in June and September. The first winner was PC G.W. Barker of Eardisley, who also had first place for his flower garden, with PC A.H. Cousins and Inspector D.A. Pickard in second and third places. The Vegetable Garden prize was won by PC S.G. Perks with Sergeant A. Moss and Superintendent A. Lewis in second and third places.

Another annual challenge was the Chief Constable's First Aid Cup, for which officers competed on an individual basis. Individuals and teams also competed in other

First Aid Competitions.

The Police Choir was formed in early 1957, from an idea put forward by T.S. Davies, M.W. Burgess, A.G. Roberts, D.A. Gibson and others, which was readily agreed to by Mr. Newton, providing that it took up no police time, and there was no personal gain. Regular officers and Special Constables were invited to join, and rehearsals began, under the direction of John Wright, so that the Choir was ready to take part in the Centenary Service at the Cathedral in April 1957. Times have changed from the early days when the choir was made up solely of police personnel, but the Annual Celebrity Concert is still an important date in the calendar.

(Photograph reproduced by courtesy of Derek Evans, ARPS, FRSA.)

Back Row,L. to R: ? Watkins, A. Benbow, J. Pritchard, J.H. Whent, R.N. Lane, H. Wright.
Middle Row, L. to R: F. Lewis, B. Gradwell, G. Nunn, T.W. Button, G. Clements, A.G. Roberts, J.W.G. Densham, B.S. Williams.
Front Row, L. to R: D.A. Gibson, C.A. White, H.J. James, P.J. Burley, J. Wright, *(Conductor)*, M.W. Burgess, D.W. Evans, T.S. Davies.

Photograph reproduced by courtesy of Derek Evans, ARPS, FRSA.

Some members of the newly formed Choir at rehearsal, early in 1957, conducted by John Wright.
A tape recording was made by Ted Daw.

Celebrity Concert at the Shire Hall, Hereford, 11th March 1965.
Back row, L. to R: PC 33 M.W. Kidd, Sgt. 44 G.R. Gough, Sgt. 24 H.L. Watkins, SC J. Podmore, PCs 43 W.T. Walker, 56 R.C. Wood, 139 P. Bristow, 73 J.W.G. Densham, 118 D.W. Mauvan, Cadet G.W. Corfield, PS 138 A. Roberts, PCs 95 S. Humphries, 36 G.T. Lewis, S/Insp. A.J.T. Richards, S/Sgt. H. Evans, S/Sgt. W. Kitson.
Middle row, L. to R: Sgt.10 B.S. Williams, PC 122 C.A. White, Sgt.146 D.W. Evans, PCs 52 C.H.W. Maddy, 11 R.N. Lane, Cadet A. Howls, S/Sgt. H. Wright, Cadet B. Smith, PC 120 S.E. Baggett, SC T. Vaughan, S/Sgt. J. Nosworthy, RPSgt. C. Evans, Sgt. 23 G.D. Surrell.
Front row, L. to R: Chief Constable R. McCartney, Mr.R. Fisher, *(Accompanist)*, Mr. J. Heddle Nash, Miss Joy Evans, Mr. E. Sanders, *(Conductor)*, Miss Tessa Robbins, Mr. J. Blair, Ch/Insp. D.A. Gibson.

Photograph reproduced by courtesy of Donovan C. Wilson, Photography.

The Herefordshire Constabulary Football Team, who played Birmingham City Police, in 1930.
Back row, L. to R: Supt. G.T. Brierley, G. Christopher, E.E. Bendall, C.R. Moody, E.C. Wills, A. Moss, T. Craig, Insp. J. Edge.
Front row, L. to R: E. Jarrett, F.J. Griffin, H.J. James, D. Grigg, E.R.P. Watkins.

Below: The successful football squad – Winners of the No. 8 District Football Trophy in 1951
Back row, L. to R: J. Keyte, A.G. Roberts, T.H. Stevens, D. Strang.
Middle row, L. to R: N. Oxlade, W.J. Hillstead, A.H. Cousins, R.N. Lane, C. Joyce, R. Colwell, D. Massam.
Seated, L. to R: T.S. Davies, K.J. Hursey, L.H. Jones, DCC T.B. Wheeler, CC F. Newton, R.C. Short, W. Wallace, P. Bristow.

Back row, L. to R: N.G. Ovens, N. Oxlade, S.G. Perks, D.H. Roberts, R.G. Kendle, G. Painter, L. Workman.
Seated, L. to R: J.R.I. Clinton, T. Batho, DCC T.B. Wheeler, CC F. Newton, R.J. Garrett, J. Keyte.

CRICKET TEAMS.

Below, Back row, L. to R: J.A.M. Main, K.J. Hursey, R.J.B. Phillips, A.W.C. Morris, R.C. Short, D. Young, T. Batho.
Seated, L. to R: L. Kedward, R.J. Garrett, G.T. Warley, D. Massam, T.H. Stevens.

(Photograph reproduced by courtesy of Derek Evans, ARPS, FRSA).

PC 132 A.J.F. Buttriss,
with his National Trophy, and individual awards for Shot-putt and Discus,
in his record-breaking year, 1963.

Herefordshire Constabulary Rugby Union Team, 1967, pictured after their first winning game, against Worcestershire Constabulary.
Back row, L. to R: B.S. Humphreys, G.S. Millichip, M.J. Moxham, *(Captain),* L. Davies, R. Powell, D.J.T. Talbot, R. Morris, D.C.S. Carter, J. Jones, A.W.C. Morris.
Front, L. to R: A. Howls, J. Maddrell, P. Warren, R.A. Hanks, J. Davies, C.H.J. Day.

INDEX

Extra to Index: Appointees 1857, Page 6; Centenary Photograph, 1957, Page 153; Nominal Roll, 30th. September 1967, Pages 63 and 64.

Numbers in Italics refer to Collar Numbers,where applicable.

INDEX

Extra to Index: Appointees 1857, Page 6; Centenary Photograph, 1957, Page 153; Nominal Roll, 30th. September 1967, Pages 63 and 64.

Numbers in Italics refer to Collar Numbers,where applicable.

INDEX

Extra to Index: Appointees 1857, Page 6; Centenary Photograph, 1957, Page 153; Nominal Roll, 30th. September 1967, Pages 63 and 64.

Numbers in Italics refer to Collar Numbers,where applicable.

INDEX

Extra to Index: Appointees 1857, Page 6; Centenary Photograph, 1957, Page 153; Nominal Roll, 30th. September 1967, Pages 63 and 64.

Numbers in Italics refer to Collar Numbers,where applicable.

INDEX

Extra to Index: Appointees 1857, Page 6; Centenary Photograph, 1957, Page 153; Nominal Roll, 30th. September 1967, Pages 63 and 64.

Numbers in Italics refer to Collar Numbers, where applicable.